Advanced French Vocabulary

Second Edition

Philip Horsfall

Nelson Thornes

First published in 1994 by:
Mary Glasgow Publications, an imprint of Nelson Thornes

This edition first published in 2001 by:
Nelson Thornes Ltd
Delta Place
27 Bath Road
CHELTENHAM
GL53 7TH
United Kingdom

09 10 11 12 / 15 14 13 12 11 10

A catalogue record for this book is available from the British Library

ISBN 978 0 7487 5780 0

Page make-up by Tech-Set, Gateshead, Tyne and Wear

Printed by Multivista Global Ltd

TABLE DES MATIÈRES

AVANT-PROPOS

Ce livre a pour but:

- d'élargir votre vocabulaire en regroupant ensemble des mots sur des sujets d'intérêt général.
- de vous aider à écrire des dissertations en vous fournissant des phrases utiles.
- de vous préparer pour votre examen.

Bien sûr, ce livre ne peut remplacer ni votre cahier de vocabulaire personnel où vous notez les mots que vous avez trouvés et dont vous avez besoin, ni un bon dictionnaire.

Il peut, cependant, vous rendre la vie plus facile!

Je vous souhaite bonne chance!

Abbréviations:

adj	adjective	*mpl*	masculine plural
pl	plural	*fpl*	feminine plural
m	masculine	*m/f*	masculine and feminine
f	feminine	*m/fpl*	masculine and feminine plural

Si le verbe est marqué #, cela vous signale qu'il est irrégulier.

À la fin de chaque section, une kyrielle d'adresses de sites utiles sur Internet vous est donnée pour vous aider à obtenir plus d'informations si vous en avez besoin. Vous pouvez aussi vous servir des moteurs de recherche suivants:

www.yahoo.fr

www.wanadoo.fr

www.nomade.com

www.eureka.fr.com

www.altavista.fr

www.franceguide.com

www.voila.fr/topics

LA CULTURE

LA LITTÉRATURE

action (*f*)	action
actuel/le	topical
ambigu/ë	ambiguous
anti-héros (*m*)	anti-hero
atmosphère (*f*)	mood
auteur (*m*)	author
cadre (*m*)	setting
caractère (*m*)	character, personality
chapitre (*m*)	chapter
citation (*f*)	quotation
citer	to quote
clou (*m*)	highlight
conte (*m*)	tale
contrebalancer	to offset
convaincant/e	convincing
crise (*f*) de conscience	crisis of conscience
critique (*f*)	criticism
décrire#	to describe
déroulement (*m*)	development
dilemme (*m*) moral	moral dilemma
dominer	to dominate
écrivain (*m*)	writer
émouvant/e	moving
s'enchaîner	to follow on, to be linked
état (*m*) d'âme	mood, frame of mind
évoquer	to call to mind
s'exprimer	to express oneself
extrait (*m*)	extract
faire# allusion à	to refer to
faire# figure de	to be regarded as
fidèle	accurate
s'identifier avec	to identify with
intrigue (*f*)	plot
invraisemblable	unbelievable
milieu (*m*)	environment, circle
moralité (*f*)	morals
narrateur (*m*)	narrator
œuvre (*f*)	work
paradoxal/e	paradoxical
parallèle (*m*)	parallel
passionnant/e	exciting
poète (*m*)	poet
point (*m*) culminant	climax
porter sur	to focus on
poussé/e par	motivated by
profondeur (*f*)	depth
psychologique	psychological
se rapporter à	to tie in with
réalisme (*m*)	realism
recréer	to recreate
résumé (*m*)	summary
révélateur/trice	enlightening
révéler#	to reveal
roman (*m*)	novel

romancier/ière (*m/f*)	*novelist*
sentiment (*m*)	*feeling*
signification (*f*)	*meaning*
sort (*m*)	*fate*
souligner	*to stress*
spirituel/le	*witty*
stimulant/e	*thought-provoking*
sujet (*m*)	*subject matter*
susciter	*to arouse, give rise to*

symbolique	*symbolic*
tendu/e	*tense*
tiraillé/e entre	*torn between*
tragédie (*f*)	*tragedy*
trait (*m*)	*feature, trait*
traiter de	*to deal with*
se transformer	*to be a changed person*
vive	*vivid*

la peinture des caractères	*characterisation*
faire# progresser l'action	*to move the plot along*
il revient sur ce thème	*he comes back to this theme*
une étude des mœurs de	*a study of the manners/morals of*
éducation sentimentale	*romantic education*
faire# ressortir la morale	*to bring out the moral*
une composante essentielle de sa personnalité	*an essential side to his character*
notre intérêt se porte sur	*our interest focuses on*
à l'arrière-plan	*in the background*
la passion possède un pouvoir destructeur	*the power of passion is destructive*
écrit/e à la première personne	*written in the first person*
les conséquences de ses actes	*the consequences of his actions*
soutenir# l'intérêt du lecteur par	*to hold the reader's interest by*
faire# revivre une époque	*to bring an era back to life*

LE THÉÂTRE

acte (*m*)	*act*
comédien/ne (*m/f*)	*actor/actress*
décor (*m*)	*scenery*
dénouement (*m*)	*outcome, ending*
dialogue (*m*)	*dialogue*
dramaturge (*m*)	*playwright*

effet (*m*) scénique	*stage effect*
entourage (*m*)	*circle, close group of people*
incarner	*to embody*
interpréter#	*to perform*
mise (*f*) en scène	*production*
personnage (*m*)	*character, person*

7

pièce (*f*)	*play*	rôle (*m*)	*role, part*
public (*m*)	*audience*	toile (*f*) de fond	
représenter	*to portray*		*backcloth, backdrop*

se laisser entraîner par	*to let oneself be carried along by*
l'action se déroule dans	*the action takes place in*
la scène se passe à	*the scene takes place at*
le sujet essentiel de la pièce	*the play's fundamental message*
mettre# en valeur ses idées sur	*to bring out clearly his/her ideas on*
entrer en scène	*to come on stage*

LE CINÉMA

acteur/actrice (*m/f*)	*actor/actress*	intimiste	*confiding*
ambiance (*f*)	*atmosphere*	long métrage (*m*)	*feature film*
au ralenti	*in slow motion*	metteur (*m*) en scène	*director*
bande (*f*) sonore	*sound-track*	nouvelle vague (*f*)	*French New Wave cinema*
bruitage (*m*)	*sound effects*	panoramiquer	*to pan*
censure (*f*)	*censorship*	partenaires (*mpl*)	*supporting cast*
cinéphile (*m/f*)	*film lover*	plateau (*m*) de tournage	*film set*
conte (*m*) de fées	*fairy tale*	premier rôle (*m*)	*leading part*
en gros plan	*in close-up*	prise (*f*) de vue(s)	*filming, shooting*
effets (*mpl*) spéciaux	*special effects*	réalisateur (*m*)	*producer*
faire# fureur	*to be all the rage*	rôle (*m*) principal	*leading role*
figurant/e (*m/f*)	*extra*	scénariste (*m/f*)	*script-writer*
film (*m*) à gros budget	*big budget film*	scène (*f*)	*scene*
film (*m*) d'époque	*a period film*	second rôle (*m*)	*supporting part*
film (*m*) de science-fiction	*sci-fi film*	suite (*f*)	*sequel*
film (*m*) noir	*social realism thriller*	tournage (*m*)	*filming*
générique (*m*)	*credits, cast-list*	tourner	*to shoot*
infographie (*f*)	*computer graphics*	truquage (*m*)	*special effects*
s'inspirer de	*to be inspired by*	vedette (*f*)	*star*

retrouver ces thèmes dans d'autres films	*to come across these themes in other films*
l'œuvre (*f*) filmique de	*the cinematic works of*
adapté/e pour le cinéma	*adapted for the cinema*

porter un roman à l'écran	*to adapt a novel for the screen*
le film s'écarte du roman	*the film does not stick to the book*
les images de synthèse	*computer generated pictures*
remporter une récompense	*to win an award*
reconstituer l'époque	*to reconstruct the period*
un film à grand succès	*a box-office hit, a blockbuster*

LA MUSIQUE

air (*m*)	*melody*
batterie (*f*)	*percussion*
bois (*mpl*)	*woodwind*
chef (*m*) d'orchestre	*conductor*
compositeur (*m*)	*composer*
cuivres (*mpl*)	*brass instruments*
disque (*m*) compact	*CD*
folklorique	*folk*
instrument (*m*) à vent	*wind instrument*
instruments (*mpl*) à cordes	*strings*
interprétation (*f*)	*performance*
mélomane (*m/f*)	*music-lover*
musique (*f*) de fond	*background music*
opéra (*m*)	*opera*
orchestre (*m*)	*orchestra*
partition (*f*)	*score*
rave (*f*)	*rave*
répéter#	*to rehearse*
soloïste (*m/f*)	*soloist*
tournée (*f*)	*tour*
tube (*m*)	*pop hit*
virtuose (*m/f*)	*virtuoso*

comporter quatre mouvements	*to be in four movements*
avoir# un énorme succès	*to be a big hit*
être# en tête du hit-parade	*to top the charts*

LES BEAUX-ARTS

abstrait/e	*abstract*
air (*m*)	*melody*
art (*m*) contemporain	*contemporary art*
artisanat (*m*)	*arts and crafts*
arts (*mpl*) premiers	*ethnic art*
assister à	*to attend*
choquant/e	*shocking*
culture (*f*) virtuelle	*virtual culture*
curiosités (*fpl*)	*sights, features*
exposition (*f*)	*exhibition*
impressionnistes (*mpl*)	*the Impressionists*

laid/e	*ugly*	restaurer	*to restore*
mouvement (*m*) surréaliste		sacré/e	*sacred*
	surrealist movement	sculpteur (*m*)	*sculptor*
objet (*m*) d'art	*work of art*	sensibilité (*f*)	*sensitivity*
patrimoine (*m*)	*cultural heritage*	subventions (*fpl*) des arts	
peinture (*f*)	*painting*		*arts grants*
peinture (*f*) à l'huile	*oil-painting*	toile (*f*)	*canvas*
philistin/e	*low-brow*	vitraux (*mpl*)	*stained glass windows*
pinceau (*m*)	*brush*	vivant/e	*lifelike*

l'art pour l'art	*art for art's sake*
faire# des études d'art	*to study art*
l'art moderne semble dénué de sens	*modern art seems devoid of meaning*

SITES INTERNET UTILES

www.francealacarte.org.uk (le site du réseau culturel français au Royaume-Uni)

www.maison-des-ecrivains.asso.fr (site sur le rôle de l'écrivain aujourd'hui)

www.admifrance.gouv.fr (un annuaire des sites Internet français)

www.cnc.fr (centre national de la cinématographie)

www.publivore.com (des infos sur le cinéma)

www.louvre.fr (site du musée du Louvre à Paris)

www.lokace.com (accès à beaucoup de sites français)

www.giverney.org/giverney.htm (site sur Giverney et Monet)

http://www.utm.edu/departments/french/french.html (liste de sites francophones)

www.ambafrance.org/ (le service culturel de l'ambassade de France au Canada)

www.culture.gouv.fr (site de la culture française)

www.academie.fr (site de l'Académie française)

http://perso.wanadoo.fr/olivier-c/AnnuaireWeb.html (des sites utiles sur la France)

— LE MONDE DU TRAVAIL —

LE COMMERCE

achat (*m*)	*purchase*
association (*f*)	*partnership*
barrières (*fpl*) douanières	
	trade barriers
biens (*mpl*)	*goods*
carte (*f*) de fidélité	*loyalty card*
chaîne (*f*) de montage	*assembly line*
clientèle (*f*)	*customers*
code (*m*) barre	*bar code*
commander	*to order*
commerçant (*m*)	*shopkeeper*
commerce (*m*) électronique	
	e-commerce
commerce (*m*) extérieur	
	overseas trade
compétitif/ve	*competitive*
consommateur (*m*)	*consumer*
détaillant (*m*)	*retailer*
économie (*f*) globalisée	
	globalised economy
effectifs (*mpl*)	*workforce*
efficacité (*f*) commerciale	
	business efficiency
emballage (*m*)	*wrapping*
entreprise (*f*)	*firm*
exportation (*f*)	*export*
fabrication (*f*)	*manufacture*
fabriquer	*to manufacture*

facture (*f*)	*bill, invoice*
faire# faillite	*to go bankrupt*
fermeture (*f*)	*closure*
filiale (*f*)	*subsidiary office*
foire (*f*)	*trade fair*
fusionner	*to merge*
gamme (*f*) de produits	
	product range
gestion (*f*)	*management*
grande surface (*f*)	*hypermarket*
guerre (*f*) des prix	*price war*
heures (*fpl*) ouvrables	*business hours*
hiérarchie (*f*)	*company structure*
imbattable	*unbeatable*
importation (*f*)	*import*
industrie(*f*) lourde	*heavy industry*
informatiser	*to computerise*
invendable	*unsaleable*
lettre (*f*) commerciale	*business letter*
libre-échange (*m*)	*free trade*
livrer	*to deliver*
loi (*f*) du marché	*market forces*
main (*f*) d'œuvre qualifiée	
	skilled labour
marchandises (*fpl*)	*goods*
matière (*f*) première	*raw material*
mondialisation (*f*)	*globalisation*
monopole (*m*)	*monopoly*

multinationale (*f*)
multinational company

petit commerçant (*m*)
small shopkeeper

point (*m*) de vente — *sales outlet*

productivité (*f*) — *productivity*

produit (*m*) — *product*

promotion (*f*) — *special offer*

protectionnisme (*m*) — *protectionism*

rabais (*m*) — *reduction*

réclamation (*f*) — *complaint*

relations (*fpl*) industrielles
industrial relations

rembourser — *to refund*

restructuration (*f*) — *restructuring*

secteur (*m*) tertiaire — *service industries*

service (*m*) après-vente
after-sales service

siège (*m*) — *headquarters*

subvention (*f*) — *subsidy*

succursale (*f*) — *branch*

technicisé/e — *high-tech*

téléachat (*m*) — *TV shopping*

vente (*f*) en gros — *wholesale trade*

vente (*f*) par correspondance
mail order selling

vente (*f*) par téléphone — *telesales*

voiture (*f*) de société — *company car*

zone (*f*) d'activités — *business park*

délaisser les commerces de quartier — *to abandon local shops*

augmenter/baisser les prix — *to increase/reduce prices*

se situer dans les zones périurbaines — *to be located on the outskirts of towns*

vérifier la date limite de vente — *to check the sell-by date*

effectuer un achat — *to make a purchase*

faire# des affaires sur une grande échelle — *to do business on a large scale*

la livraison à domicile — *home delivery*

faire# face à la concurrence — *to stand up to the competition*

répondre# aux besoins des clients — *to meet the customers' needs*

une société anonyme — *public limited company*

les affaires reprennent — *business is looking up*

les dot.com/les startups — *dot.com industries*

avec Internet une nouvelle économie s'est mise en place — *with the internet a new economy has been put in place*

offrir# un service personnalisé — *to offer a personalised service*

supprimer des emplois — *to axe jobs*

attirer des sponsors — *to attract sponsors*

la reprise économique — *the economic recovery*

redresser l'économie	*to put the economy back on its feet*
la mauvaise gestion	*mismanagement*
les industries traditionnelles	*smokestack industries*
une offre publique d'achat (OPA)	*a takeover bid*
l'économie parallèle	*the black economy*
travailler à l'étranger	*to work abroad*
les dépenses de consommation	*consumer spending*
supprimer l'intermédiaire	*to cut out the middleman*
la création de nouveaux emplois	*job creation*
produire# à plein rendement	*to be working at full capacity*
être partisan du libéralisme économique	*to be a supporter of free enterprise*

LA CHASSE À L'EMPLOI

bureau (*m*) de placement	*personnel agency*
candidat/e (*m/f*)	*applicant*
candidature (*f*)	*application*
carrière (*f*)	*career*
centre (*m*) d'orientation	*careers office*
chasseur (*m*) de tête	*headhunter*
contrat (*m*)	*contract*
curriculum (*m*) vitae	*curriculum vitae*
cursus (*m*)	*career path*
débouché (*m*)	*job opening*
demande (*f*) d'emploi	*application*
demandeur/euse (*m/f*) d'emploi	*job-hunter*
diplômé/e	*qualified*
engager	*to employ, hire*
entretien (*m*)	*interview*
entrevue (*f*)	*interview*
intérimaire	*temporary*

lacune (*f*)	*gap*
lettre (*f*) explicative	*covering letter*
nommer	*to appoint*
offre (*f*) d'emploi	*job offer*
parcours (*m*) professionnel	*professional career*
poste (*m*)	*post, position*
postulant/e (*m/f*)	*applicant*
profil (*m*) du poste	*job description*
recruter	*to recruit*
recyclage (*m*)	*retraining*
se recycler	*to retrain*
référence (*f*)	*reference*
refus (*m*)	*rejection*
service (*m*) du personnel	*personnel department*
se spécialiser	*to specialise*
stage (*m*)	*work experience*
surdiplômé/e	*overqualified*
se valoriser	*to boost your self-esteem*
visite (*f*) impromptue	*cold call*

13

un employeur qui ne fait pas de discrimination	*an equal opportunities employer*
les possibilités d'avancement	*career prospects*
un formulaire de demande d'emploi	*job application form*
fournir des références	*to act as a referee*
convoquer quelqu'un pour une entrevue	*to invite someone for an interview*
postuler pour un emploi	*to apply for a job*
poser sa candidature	*to submit one's application*
les conditions de travail	*conditions of employment*
conseiller/ère d'orientation professionnelle	*careers adviser*
exercer# une profession	*to carry out/practise a profession*
un contrat à durée déterminée	*a fixed-term contract*
un boulot cul-de-sac	*a dead-end job*
faire# carrière	*to make a career for oneself*

LES EMPLOYÉS

administratifs (*mpl*)	*admin staff*
apprenti/e (*m/f*)	*apprentice*
associé/e (*m/f*)	*partner*
cadre (*m/f*)	*executive*
chef (*m*) d'entreprise	*head of a company*
clientèle (*f*)	*customers*
collègue (*m/f*)	*colleague*
direction (*f*)	*management*
effectifs (*mpl*)	*workforce*
employé/e (*m/f*)	*employee*
employeur/euse (*m/f*)	*employer*
expert-conseil (*m*)	*consultant*
fabricant/e (*m/f*)	*manufacturer*
femme (*f*) d'affaires	*businesswoman*
fonctionnaire (*m/f*)	*civil servant*
fournisseur (*m*)	*supplier*
gérant/e (*m/f*)	*manager/ess*
gestion (*f*)	*management*
heures (*fpl*) souples	*flexi-time*
homme (*m*) d'affaires	*businessman*
main (*f*) d'œuvre	*workforce*
manœuvre (*m*)	*unskilled labourer*
négociant/ière (*m/f*)	*merchant*
ouvrier/ière (*m/f*) posté/e	*shiftworker*
patron/onne (*m/f*)	*boss*
patronat (*m*)	*the employers*
personnel (*m*)	*staff*
propriétaire (*m/f*)	*owner*
représentant/e (*m/f*)	*representative*
retraite (*f*)	*pension*
secrétaire (*f*) intérimaire	*temp*
stagiaire (*mf*)	*trainee*

licencier des employés	*to lay off staff*
le président-directeur général (PDG)	*the managing director*
prendre# sa retraite	*to retire*
faire# des études commerciales	*to do business studies*
employé à son compte	*self-employed*
les préretraités	*people who have taken early retirement*
un comité d'entreprise	*staff committee*

AU BUREAU

à l'appareil	*on the line (phone)*
base (*f*) de données	*database*
bureautique (*f*)	*office automation*
classeur (*m*)	*filing cabinet*
col (*m*) blanc	*white-collar worker*
communication (*f*) interurbaine	*long-distance call*
communication pour l'étranger	*international call*
coup (*m*) de téléphone	*phone call*
courrier (*m*) électronique	*E-mail*
dossier (*m*)	*file*
espace (*m*) de travail	*office space*
fax (*m*)	*fax*
faxer	*to fax*
indicatif (*m*)	*dialling code*
machine (*f*) à écrire	*typewriter*
machine (*f*) de traitement de texte	*word processor*
numérotation (*f*) téléphonique	*telephone number system*
ordinateur (*m*) de bureau	*desktop computer*
ordinateur (*m*) portatif	*laptop*
ordre (*m*) du jour	*agenda*
par téléphone	*by telephone*
passer	*to put through (on phone)*
photocopieuse (*f*)	*photocopier*
poste (*m*)	*extension*
portable (*m*)	*mobile phone*
raccrocher	*to hang up (phone)*
rappeler#	*to call back (phone)*
renseignements (*mpl*)	*Directory Enquiries*
répondeur (*m*) automatique	*answerphone*
standard (*m*)	*switchboard*
télé-travail (*m*)	*teleworking*
télécopie (*f*)	*fax (message)*
télécopieur (*m*)	*fax machine*
téléphone (*m*) cellulaire	*cellular phone*
téléphone (*m*) portatif	*mobile phone*
ticket (*m*)	*luncheon voucher*
travail (*m*) administratif	*paperwork*

le travail à plein temps n'est plus la norme	*full-time working is no longer the norm*
toucher €900 par mois	*to be paid 900 Euros a month*
la ligne est occupée	*the line's engaged*
ne quittez pas	*hold the line*
vous êtes en ligne	*you're through (on phone)*
téléphoner à l'extérieur	*to make an outside call*
appeler# par l'automatique	*to dial direct*
faire# un faux numéro	*to dial a wrong number*
avoir# des heures de bureau	*to work office hours*

AU TRAVAIL

année (*f*) sabbatique	*sabbatical year*
avancement (*m*)	*promotion*
avantage (*m*) annexe	*fringe benefit*
blocage (*m*) des salaires	*wage freeze*
boulot (*m*)	*work*
bulletin (*m*) de paie	*payslip*
bureaucratie (*f*)	*bureaucracy*
caisse (*f*) de retraite	*pension scheme*
collaboration (*f*)	*teamwork*
congé (*m*) de maternité	*maternity leave*
congé (*m*) de paternité	*paternity leave*
congés (*mpl*) payés	*paid holidays*
crèche (*f*)	*crèche*
démission (*f*)	*resignation*
départ (*m*) volontaire	*voluntary redundancy*
employer	*to employ*
feuille (*f*) de paie	*payslip*
frais (*mpl*) de voyage	*travel expenses*
heures (*fpl*) supplémentaires	*overtime*
horaire (*m*) variable	*flexi-time*
indépendant/e	*self-employed*
jour (*m*) férié	*bank holiday*
licenciement (*m*)	*redundancy*
métier (*m*)	*trade, profession*
partage (*m*) de poste	*job-sharing*
période (*f*) probatoire	*probationary period*
petit bénéfice (*m*)	*perk*
préretraite (*f*)	*early retirement*
rémunération (*f*)	*payment*
rendez-vous (*m*)	*appointment*
responsabilité (*f*)	*responsibility*
réunion (*f*)	*meeting*
salaire (*m*) minimum (SMIC)	*minimum wage*
salarié/e (*m/f*)	*wage-earner*
service (*m*)	*department*
syndicaliste (*m/f*)	*trade union member*
syndicat (*m*)	*trade union*
tâche (*f*)	*task*
traitement (*m*)	*salary*

travail (*m*) à mi-temps	*part-time work*
travail (*m*) à plein temps	*full-time work*
travail (*m*) au noir	*moonlighting*

travail (*m*) en équipe	*shiftwork*
voiture (*f*) de fonction	*company car*
voyage (*m*) d'affaires	*business trip*

faire# des affaires avec quelqu'un	*to do business with someone*
la sécurité de l'emploi	*job security*
la satisfaction au travail	*job satisfaction*
la formation sur le tas	*on-the-job training*
travailler à son propre compte	*to be self-employed*
donner son congé	*to hand in your notice*
travailler à domicile	*to work from home*
partir# en préretraite	*to take early retirement*
la CGT (Confédération générale du travail)	*main French trade union*
faire# partie d'un syndicat	*to belong to a union*
la semaine des 35 heures	*the 35-hour week*
un conflit salarial	*a wage dispute*
réclamer une augmentation de salaire	*to put in for a pay rise*
le mouvement de grève	*strike action*
une demande irréaliste	*an unrealistic demand*
faire# les trois-huit	*to work around the clock*
promouvoir# l'égalité des chances	*to promote equal opportunities*
la retraite de base	*basic state pension*
la retraite complémentaire	*company pension*
les droits des travailleurs	*workers' rights*
donner son préavis	*to hand in one's notice*

LA BANQUE

agence (*f*)	*branch*
argent (*m*) liquide	*cash*
brut	*gross*
carte (*f*) à puce	*smart card*

Carte (*f*) Bleue	*Visa card*
carte (*f*) de crédit	*credit card*
carte (*f*) de retrait	*cashcard*
compte (*m*) courant	*current account*
compte (*m*) d'épargne	*savings account*

découvert (m)	overdraft	hypothèque (f)	mortgage
devises (fpl)	foreign currency	intérêts (mpl)	interest
directeur (m) d'agence		net	net
	bank manager	prêt (m) bancaire	bank loan
distributeur (m) automatique de billets		relevé (m) de compte	statement
	cash dispenser	retirer	to withdraw
emprunt (m)	loan	secteur (m) bancaire	banking industry
épargnant/e (m/f)	saver	société (f) sans argent	
espèces (fpl)	cash		cashless society
frais (mpl) de banque	banking charges	virer	to transfer

encaisser/toucher un chèque	to cash a cheque
verser de l'argent sur un compte	to pay money into an account
le taux de change	exchange rate
le taux d'intérêt	the interest rate
atteindre# son niveau le plus bas	to reach an all-time low
fairé# un emprunt	to borrow money
le blanchiment de l'argent	money laundering
effectuer un virement bancaire	to carry out a credit transfer

LES FINANCES

action (f)	share	conjoncture (f)	state of the economy
actionnaire (m/f)	shareholder	contribuable (m/f)	taxpayer
s'autofinancer	to be self-financing	crise (f)	crisis
bénéfice (m)	profit	dette (f) (publique)	(national) debt
blocage (m) des prix	price freeze	dépense (f)	expenditure
boom (m)	boom	effondrement (m)	slump
bourse (f)	stock exchange	endetté/e	in debt
budget (m)	budget	financement (m)	finance
charge (f) fiscale	tax burden	fiscalité (f)	taxation
chiffre (m) d'affaires	turnover	forces (fpl) du marché	market forces
		fraude (f) fiscale	tax evasion

hausse (*f*) des prix	*price rise*	privatiser	*to privatise*
impôt (*m*) sur le revenu	*income tax*	prix (*m*) de revient	*cost price*
inflationniste	*inflationary*	prix (*mpl*) des actions	*share prices*
krach (*m*)	*stock-market crash*	récession (*f*)	*recession*
libre-échange (*m*)	*free-trade*	recettes (*fpl*) fiscales	*tax revenue*
milliard (*m*)	*billion*	reçu (*m*)	*receipt*
passage (*m*) à la baisse	*downward trend*	rentabilité (*f*)	*profitability*
perception (*f*)	*tax office*	SMIC (*m*)	*minimum wage*
perspectives (*fpl*)	*prospects*	spéculer	*to speculate*
placement (*m*)	*investment*	surchauffe (*f*)	*overheating*
placer	*to invest*	système (*m*) fiscal	*tax system*
politique (*f*) de rigueur	*austerity measures*	taux (*m*) d'inflation	*rate of inflation*
		TVA (*f*)	*VAT*
pourcentage (*m*)	*percentage*	valeur (*f*) marchande	*market value*

donner du tonus à l'économie	*to boost the economy*
le mécanisme de change	*the exchange rate mechanism*
réduire# le déficit budgétaire	*to reduce the budget deficit*
la relance économique	*the economic revival*
favoriser la croissance	*to encourage growth*
baisser/augmenter les impôts	*to lower/increase taxes*
le cours des actions est monté	*the share price has risen*
les exportations invisibles	*invisible exports*
les marchés financiers	*financial markets*
le déficit commercial	*the trade gap*
la balance des paiements	*the balance of payments*
la balance commerciale	*the balance of trade*
les résultats financiers	*trade figures*
l'indice du coût de la vie	*the cost of living index*
un délit d'initié	*insider dealing*
la bourse est en baisse/hausse	*the stock market is going down/up*

SITES INTERNET UTILES

www.banque-france.fr (site de la banque de France)

www.afb.fr (site de l'association française des banques)

www.admifrance.gouv.fr (un annuaire des sites Internet français)

http://finance.club-internet.fr (des infos sur les bourses et les entreprises)

www.force-ouvriere.fr (site de la Confédération Générale du Travail)

http://globegate.utm.edu/french/topics/finance.html (beaucoup d'information sur les banques et le commerce)

www.pratique.fr (site sur l'euro)

http://globegate.utm.edu/french/globegate_mirror/emploi.html (site sur les emplois)

www.francealacarte.org.uk (le site du réseau culturel français au Royaume-Uni)

www.bruxelles-j.be/index.htm (information jeunesse sur la formation et le travail)

www.information-jeunesse.tm.fr (centre d'information et de documentation jeunesse)

http://perso.wanadoo.fr/olivier-c/AnnuaireWeb.html (des sites sur le commerce)

L'ENSEIGNEMENT

L'EDUCATION

absentéisme (*m*)	*truancy*
agression (*f*)	*attack*
année (*f*) scolaire	*the academic year*
assidu/e	*hard-working*
bonne conduite (*f*)	*good behaviour*
bulletin (*m*) scolaire	*report*
chahuter	*to run riot*
chaîne (*f*) éducative	*educational channel*
classe-poubelle (*f*)	*sink group*
collégien/ne (*m/f*)	*pupil*
connaissance (*f*)	*knowledge*
cours (*m*) particulier	*private lesson*
directeur/trice (*m/f*)	*headteacher*
discipline (*f*)	*discipline*
en première	*in Year 12*
en terminale	*in Year 13*
école (*f*) libre	*private school*
école (*f*) publique	*state school*
élitisme (*m*)	*elitism*
illettré/e	*illiterate*
indiscipliné/e	*badly behaved*
internat (*m*)	*boarding school*
lycée (*m*) professionnel	*secondary school for vocational training*
mixte	*mixed*
obligatoire	*compulsory*
pédagogique	*educational*
pensionnat (*m*)	*boarding school*
périscolaire	*extracurricular*
pluridisciplinaire	*cross-curricular*
programme (*m*) scolaire	*curriculum*
rattraper	*to catch up*
redoubler	*to repeat a year*
renvoyé/e	*suspended, expelled*
réunion (*f*) de profs	*staff meeting*
sagesse (*f*)	*good behaviour*
scolariser	*to send to school*
scolarité (*f*)	*schooling*
sortie (*f*) scolaire	*school trip*
surveillant/e (*m/f*)	*supervisor*
ZEP (*f*)	*educational priority zone*

l'enseignement laïque	*state education*
la formation est la clé de l'avenir	*education is the key to the future*
le système éducatif	*the educational system*
une dégradation des niveaux	*a drop in standards*
prolonger# la scolarité	*to raise the school-leaving age*

le taux d'encadrement	*the staff-pupil ratio*
la pesanteur administrative	*the administrative burden*
le programme d'enseignement obligatoire	*the national curriculum*
l'âge de la fin de la scolarité	*school-leaving age*
le premier cycle	*education from 11–13*
le second cycle court	*education from 14–16*
les activités extra-scolaires	*out of school activities*
l'état des locaux	*the state of the buildings*
alléger les programmes	*to lighten the curriculum*
les agressions au collège augmentent	*violence at school is on the increase*
une matière obligatoire/facultative	*a compulsory/optional subject*
faire# l'école buissonnière	*to play truant*
les classes surchargées	*overcrowded classrooms*
un programme trop chargé	*an overloaded curriculum*

LES EXAMENS

appréciation (*f*)	*assessment*
baccalauréat (*m*)	*A-level equivalent*
bachelier/ière (*m/f*)	*someone who has the 'bac'*
bachoter	*to swot, cram*
concours (*m*)	*competition*
contrôle (*m*) continu	*continuous assessment*
échec (*m*)	*failure*
échouer à	*to fail*
épreuve (*f*)	*test*
équitable	*fair*
interrogation (*f*)	*test*
oral/e	*oral, verbal*
passer un examen	*to take an exam*
pratique	*practical*
résultat (*m*)	*result*
réussir à	*to pass*
réussir ses études	*to do well in one's studies*
la réussite scolaire	*academic success*
réviser	*to revise*
sélectionner	*to select*
théorique	*theoretical*
tricher	*to cheat*

le bac est le sésame à la faculté	*the 'bac' is the key to a university place*
avoir# un trou de mémoire	*to have your mind go blank*
la sélection par l'échec	*to weed out by examination*

se sentir# bloqué/e	*to have a mental block*
décrocher le bac	*to gain the 'bac'*
les diplômes scolaires	*educational qualifications*
faire# trop pression sur quelqu'un	*to put someone under too much pressure*
avoir# mention passable/assez bien/ bien/très bien	*to get a grade D/C/B/A*
les élèves sous-performants	*underachievers*

APRÈS LE LYCEE

amphithéâtre (*m*)	*lecture hall*
année (*f*) sabbatique	*gap-year*
approfondir	*to deepen*
bourse (*f*)	*grant*
CAPES (*m*)	*teaching diploma*
club (*m*) des étudiants	*students' union*
cours (*m*)	*lecture*
cours (*m*) du soir	*evening class*
se cultiver	*to improve one's mind*
cursus (*m*)	*degree course*
diplôme (*m*)	*qualification*
diplômé/e	*qualified*
directeur/trice (*m/f*) d'études	*tutor*
doctorat (*m*)	*Ph.D.*
École polytechnique (*f*)	*specialist college*
égalité (*f*) des chances	*equal opportunities*
faculté (*f*)	*university*
formation (*f*)	*training*
Grandes Écoles (*fpl*)	*prestigious, specialist universities*
s'instruire#	*to educate oneself*
licence (*f*)	*degree*
licencié/e (*m/f*)	*graduate*
maîtrise (*f*)	*MA*
orientation (*f*)	*careers advice*
recherche (*f*)	*research*
semestre (*m*)	*semester*
stage (*m*)	*training course*
stagiaire (*m/f*)	*trainee*
thèse (*f*)	*thesis*
travaux (*mpl*) dirigés	*tutorial*
trimestre (*m*)	*term*
universitaire	*university (adj)*

la cité universitaire	*hall of residence*
poursuivre# ses études	*to continue with one's studies*
faire# cours sur	*to lecture on*

la formation pédagogique	*teacher training*
la formation en alternance	*sandwich course*
s'inscrire# à un cours	*to register for a course*
le concours d'entrée à	*competitive entrance examination for*
une classe préparatoire	*group preparing for entrance exams*
l'école normale supérieure	*specialist teacher training college*
une formation professionnelle	*vocational training*

LA VIE AU PAIR

accepter	*to accept*
s'adapter	*to settle down*
âge (*m*) minimum	*minimum age*
agence (*f*) au pair	*au pair agency*
aide (*f*) maternelle	*mother's help*
avoir# charge de	*to be in charge of*
avoir# droit à	*to be entitled to*
certificat (*m*) médical	*medical certificate*
conditions (*fpl*)	*requirements*
conditions (*fpl*) de travail	*working conditions*
connaissance (*f*) de langues	*language skills*
conseils (*mpl*)	*advice*
convenable	*suitable*
défrayer# quelqu'un	*to meet someone's expenses*
durée (*f*)	*duration*
essentiel/le	*essential*
expérimenté/e	*experienced*
faire# du babysitting	*to babysit*

fille (*f*) demi pair	*part-time au pair*
formulaire (*m*) de demande	*application form*
frais (*m*)	*expenses*
garder	*to watch over*
habituel/le	*routine*
jour (*m*) de congé	*day off*
lettre (*f*) de recommandation	*letter of recommendation*
logement (*m*) gratuit	*free lodgings*
obligeant/e	*helpful*
occasion (*f*)	*opportunity*
s'occuper de	*to look after*
pension (*f*) gratuite	*free board*
perfectionner	*to practise, to improve*
placement (*m*)	*position, post*
préavis (*m*)	*advance notice*
quotidien/ne	*daily*
responsable de	*responsible for*
séjour (*m*)	*stay*
sérieux/euse	*reliable*
les tâches (*fpl*) ménagères	*household tasks*

suivre# des cours	*to attend classes*
perfectionner son français	*to practise/improve one's French*
se déclarer à la police	*to register with the police*
être# d'un grand secours	*to be very helpful*
nous exigeons deux références	*we require two references*
écrire# pour confirmer ces dispositions	*to write to confirm these arrangements*
un coupon-réponse international	*an international reply coupon*
s'arranger# avec quelqu'un pour faire quelque chose	*to arrange with someone to do something*
les modalités d'occupations	*the details of the work to be done*
être# en règle avec les autorités	*to have one's papers in order with the authorities*
prendre# les repas en commun	*to have meals with the family*
recevoir# une rétribution de	*to receive a payment of*
recevoir# de l'argent de poche	*to receive pocket money*

SITES INTERNET UTILES

www.lokace.com (accès à beaucoup de sites français)

http://citizens.eu.int/fr/fr/fr/origdest.htm (renseignements concernant les études et l'égalité des chances en France)

www.admifrance.gouv.fr (un annuaire des sites Internet français)

www.francealacarte.org.uk (le site du réseau culturel français au Royaume-Uni)

www.cndp.fr/ (site des centres de documentation pédagogique)

www.utm.edu/departments/french/french.html (grande liste de sites francophones)

www.pratique.fr (sites sur la scolarité et la formation)

www.information-jeunesse.tm.fr/ (centre d'information et de documentation jeunesse)

www.bruxelles-j.be/index.htm (site d'information jeunesse sur l'enseignement)

www.education.gouv.fr (site du ministère de l'éducation nationale en France)

http://perso.wanadoo.fr/olivier-c/AnnuaireWeb.html (adresses sur l'enseignement)

www.alegria.fr/fr/enfant/pair.htm (des infos sur les jeunes filles au pair)

www.accueil-international.com/index.htm (placements au pair en France)

www.aupair.ch/frichtli.html (des infos pour jeunes filles au pair en Suisse)

L'ENVIRONNEMENT

LE TRANSPORT

aérien/ne	air (adj)
Alcootest (m)	Breathalyser
annulation (f)	cancellation
atterrir	to land
automobiliste (m/f)	motorist
avion (m) à réaction	jet aircraft
blocus (m)	blockade
bouchon (m)	traffic jam
bruyant/e	noisy
capacité (f)	capacity
carambolage (m)	pile up
carlingue (f)	aircraft cabin
ceinture (f) de sécurité	seatbelt
charter (m)	charter flight
chauffard (m)	roadhog
chemin (m) de fer	railway
cheminots (mpl)	rail workers
circulation (f)	traffic
circuler	to run
code (m) de la route	highway code
compagnie (f) aérienne	airline
contraignant/e	restricting
contravention (f)	fine
couloir (m) de bus	bus lane
co-voiturage (m)	car sharing
décoller	to take off
décongestionner	to relieve congestion
délai (m)	delay
se déplacer	to get around
désaffecté/e	disused
économique	fuel-efficient
efficace	efficient
embouteillage (m)	traffic jam
excès (m) de vitesse	speeding
faire# de l'autostop	to hitch-hike
ferroviaire	railway (adj)
garer	to park
grands axes (mpl)	main roads
heures (fpl) de pointe	rush hours
horaire (m)	timetable
incommode	inconvenient
limite (f) de vitesse	speed limit
long-courrier	long-haul (aircraft)
mal (m) de l'air	airsickness
navette (f)	shuttle
péage (m)	toll
périphérique (m)	ring road
permis (m) de conduire	driving licence
perturbateur/trice	disruptive
piste (f) cyclable	cycle lane
poids (m) lourd	heavy goods vehicle
rame (f)	underground train
rapidité (f)	speed
relier	to link
retardé/e	delayed
réseau (m) autoroutier	motorway network

rocade (*f*)	*bypass/ringroad*
rouler	*to drive along*
routier (*m*)	*lorry driver*
rues (*fpl*) piétonnes	
	pedestrianised streets
sécurité (*f*) routière	*road safety*
sous-investissement (*m*)	
	underinvestment

subvention (*f*)	*subsidy*
trajet (*m*)	*journey*
se véhiculer	*to get around*
voiture (*f*) particulière	*private car*
zone (*f*) piétonne	
	pedestrian precinct

emprunter les transports en commun	*to use public transport*
une ville bien desservie	*a town with a good transport system*
le parc (*m*) automobile	*the number of vehicles on the road*
rétrécir les distances	*to shrink distances*
un investissement dans l'infrastructure	*an investment in the infrastructure*
l'hécatombe sur les routes	*the carnage on the roads*
une autoroute à trois voies	*a three lane motorway*
un gros embouteillage	*gridlock*
des systèmes de transport surchargés	*overloaded transport systems*
l'ensemble de la France	*the whole of France*
faire une virée en voiture	*to go for a ride in the car*

L'ÉNERGIE

approvisionner en	*to supply with*
carburant (*m*)	*fuel*
centrale (*f*) nucléaire	
	nuclear power station
charbon (*m*)	*coal*
combustible (*m*) organique	*biofuel*
combustibles (*mpl*) fossiles	
	fossil fuels
déchets (*m*) nucléaires	*nuclear waste*
désactiver	*to deactivate*
diversifier	*to diversify*

économies (*f*) d'énergie	
	energy savings
énergie (*f*) éolienne	*wind power*
énergie (*f*) solaire	*solar power*
éolienne (*f*)	*wind farm*
houille (*f*) blanche	
	hydro-electric power
inépuisable	*inexhaustible*
isolation (*f*)	*insulation*
isoler	*to insulate*
panneau (*m*) solaire	*solar panel*
politique (*f*) énergétique	
	energy policy

problème (*m*) énergétique
the energy problem

radio-actif/ve *radioactive*

remplacer *to replace*

ressources (*f*) naturelles
natural resources

trouver des énergies douces *to find safe energy sources*

des énergies (*f*) renouvelables *renewable energy sources*

enrayer# la menace nucléaire *to stop the nuclear threat*

répondre# aux besoins énergétiques *to meet the energy requirements*

provenir# du nucléaire *to come from nuclear energy*

utilisé/e à des fins pacifiques *used for peaceful purposes*

risque (*m*) nucléaire *nuclear risk*

surgénérateur (*m*)
fast breeder reactor

usine (*f*) marémotrice
tidal power station

LA POLLUTION ET LA CONSERVATION

biodégradable *biodegradable*

biosphère (*f*) *biosphere*

bombe (*f*) aérosol *aerosol spray*

brique (*f*) *carton*

broyeur (*m*) d'ordures
waste disposal unit

calotte (*f*) glaciaire *icecap*

CFC (*mpl*) *CFCs*

consigne (*f*) *deposit*

contaminé/e *contaminated*

conteneur (*m*) vert *bottle bank*

contribuable (*m*) *taxpayer*

couche (*f*) d'ozone *ozone layer*

coûts (*mpl*) de collecte
collection costs

déboiser *to deforest*

décharge (*f*) *dump*

déchets (*mpl*) *waste, refuse*

déchetterie (*f*) *waste disposal site*

se décomposer *to decompose*

défenseur (*m*) de la nature
conservationist

défricher *to clear (for cultivation)*

dépotoire (*m*) *rubbish tip*

désertification (*f*)
turning into a desert

eaux (*fpl*) de baignade *bathing water*

éboueur (*m*) *refuse collector*

écolabel (*m*) *label showing a product is environmentally friendly*

écolo *green*

écologiste (*m/f*) *environmentalist*

écologique *ecological*

effet (*m*) de serre *greenhouse effect*

élimination (*f*) des déchets
waste disposal

emballage (*m*) *packaging*

engrais (m) chimique	artificial fertiliser
épuration (f)	purification
essence (f) sans plomb	lead-free petrol
étiquetage (m)	labelling
fioul (m)	fuel-oil
gaspiller	to waste
gaz (m) carbonique	carbon dioxide
gestion (f) des déchets	waste management
insonoriser	to soundproof
jetable	disposable
logo (m) vert	green label
marée (f) noire	large oil slick
nappe (f) de pétrole	small oil slick
nettoyage (m)	clean-up
ordures (fpl) ménagères	household waste
oxyde (m) de carbone	carbon monoxide
papier (m) recyclé	recycled paper
pluie (f) acide	acid rain
polluant	polluting
polluer	to pollute
pollution (f) des eaux	water pollution
pot (m) catalytique	catalytic converter
produit (m) bio(logique)	organically grown product
ramassage (m) d'ordures	refuse collection
rayons (mpl) ultraviolets	ultra-violet rays
se réchauffer	to heat up
récif (m) coralien	coral reef
récupérable	reclaimable
récupération (f)	salvaging, reprocessing
recyclable	recyclable
régions (fpl) boisées	woodlands
renouvelable	renewable
réutilisable	reusable
site (m) vierge	green-field site
tas (m) de compost	compost heap
toxique	poisonous
trier	to separate out
usine (f) de traitement	recycling plant
usine (f) d'incinération	incineration plant
vicié/e	polluted
vidanges (fpl)	sewage

les dépôts sauvages	illegal tipping
l'aménagement de l'environnement	managing the environment
une bouteille consignée	a bottle with a deposit
la dépollution des plages	cleaning up the beaches
le réchauffement de la terre	global warming
le climat est soumis à	the climate is subject to

le changement climatique	*climatic change*
avoir# des conséquences redoutables	*to have dreadful consequences*
une lessive aux enzymes	*a biological washing powder*
défricher les forêts tropicales	*to cut down the rainforests*
les glaces polaires fondent	*the polar ice-caps are melting*
le niveau des océans monte	*the sea-level is rising*
le phosphate asphyxie les rivières	*phosphates are choking the rivers*
les rejets de carbone des voitures	*carbon emissions from cars*
qui ne nuit pas à l'environnement	*environmentally friendly*
dégrader l'environnement	*to damage the environment*
un risque pour la santé	*a health hazard*
les questions écologiques	*green issues*
un groupe de pression écologiste	*environmental pressure group*
un défenseur de l'environnement	*an environmentalist*
les Amis de la Terre	*Friends of the Earth*
faire# prendre conscience aux gens	*to raise people's awareness*
la croissance démographique	*the growth in population*
les nappes d'eaux souterraines	*underground water tables*
les matières premières	*raw materials*
perturber l'écosystème	*to upset the ecosystem*
l'évacuation des vidanges	*sewage disposal*
faire# rimer l'écologie et l'économie	*to mix the environment and the economy sensibly*

LES DROITS DES ANIMAUX

abandonner	*to abandon*
abattoir (*m*)	*slaughterhouse*
agoniser	*to be dying*
anesthésier	*to anaesthetise*
animaux (*mpl*) de boucherie	*fatstock, animals killed for meat*

s'apitoyer sur	*to feel pity for*
atroce	*atrocious*
baleine (*f*)	*whale*
bébé-phoque (*m*)	*baby seal*
braconnage (*m*)	*poaching*
chasse (*f*)	*hunting*
cible (*f*)	*target*
cobaye (*m*)	*guinea pig (in experiment)*

dompter	to tame		guetter	to lie in wait for
dresser	to train		humain/e	humane
élevage (m)	rearing, breeding		mammifère (m)	mammal
extinction (f)	extinction		menacer#	to threaten
faune (f)	wildlife		piéger#	to trap
filets (mpl) dérivants	drift nets		rage (f)	rabies
fourrure (f)	fur		sport (m) sanguinaire	blood-sport
gibier (m)	game		vivisection (f)	vivisection

la cruauté envers les animaux	cruelty to animals
le commerce illégal de l'ivoire	the illegal trade in ivory
l'expérimentation animale	experiments on animals
la chasse baleinière commerciale	commercial whaling
le défenseur des droits des animaux	animal rights activist
la préservation de la baleine	saving the whale
les espèces menacées	threatened species
infliger# des souffrances à	to inflict suffering on
préconiser l'arrêt total de	to be in favour of a total ban on
l'expérience médicale	medical experiment
une atteinte aux droits des animaux	an infringement of animal rights
être# en voie de disparition	to be close to extinction
les animaux dans leur milieu naturel	animals in their natural surroundings

SITES INTERNET UTILES

www.union-fin.fr/natcog/lexique/lexique.html (lexique de l'écologie)

www.admifrance.gouv.fr (un annuaire des sites Internet français)

www.citeweb.net/carbu/ (des infos sur la pollution automobile)

www.pratique.fr (sites sur le transport)

www.grolier.fr/studio (des infos sur le transport)

http://metropolitain.citeweb.net/index.html (tout sur le métro parisien) www.agora21.org/fiches/fne.html (France Nature Environnement)

www.chez.com/geres (groupe énergies renouvelables et environnement)

www.ifen.fr/ree/couv.htm (institut français de l'environnement)

www.mrn.gouv.qc.ca/2/intro.asp (l'énergie au Québec)

http://perso.wanadoo.fr/recupyl (site sur le recyclage)

http://assoc.wanadoo.fr/vertsdordogne (les verts et l'écologie en Dordogne)

www.ecolo.org (association des écologistes pour le nucléaire)

www.sortirdunucleaire.org (site anti-nucléaire)

www.fostplus.be/st/code/fr/index.htm (des infos sur le recyclage)

www.geocities.com/RainForest/Vines/3473 (des infos sur l'effet de serre etc. – regardez les 99 réponses sur l'environnement de l'Académie de Montpellier)

www.ec.gc.ca/ (le site d'Environnement Canada)

www.pmaf.org (protection mondiale des animaux de ferme)

www.spa.asso.fr (société protectrice des animaux)

LES ÉTRANGERS

LES GENS

allogène	*non-native*
autochtone	*native*
Beur (*m*)	*second generation North African immigrant*
cohabitation (*f*)	*living together*
concitoyen/ne (*m/f*)	*fellow citizen*
étranger/ère (*m/f*)	*foreigner*
habitants (*mpl*) du pays	*resident population*
immigrant/e (*m/f*)	*immigrant*
immigré/e (*m/f*)	*immigrant*

indigène	*local, indigenous*
Maghrébin/e (*m/f*)	*North African*
personnes (*fpl*) de couleur	*black and Asian people*
population (*f*) de couleur	*black and Asian population*
réfugié/e (*m/f*)	*refugee*
ressortissant/e (*m/f*)	*national*
sans-papiers (*m*)	*illegal immigrant*
société (*f*) pluriculturelle	*multicultural society*
visiteur/euse (*m/f*)	*visitor*

le brassage de races	*the intermixing of races*
un groupe ethnique minoritaire	*an ethnic minority*
les immigrés clandestins	*illegal immigrants*
vivre# en harmonie	*to live together harmoniously*
un Français à part entière	*a fully-fledged French citizen*
les immigrés de la deuxième génération	*second-generation immigrants*
se sentir# mal à l'aise	*to feel ill at ease*

L'IMMIGRATION

ascension (*f*) sociale	*social advancement*
asile (*m*) politique	*political asylum*
assimilation (*f*)	*absorption*
camp (*m*) de réfugiés	*refugee camp*
carte (*f*) de séjour	*residence permit*
carte (*f*) de travail	*work permit*

chercher asile	*to seek asylum*
choc (*m*) culturel	*culture shock*
cité (*f*) de transit	*temporary hostel*
citoyenneté (*f*)	*citizenship*
demandeur (*m*) d'asile	*asylum seeker*
désorienté/e	*bewildered*
en règle	*in order*
s'entr'aider	*to help each other*

ethnique	*ethnic*	Maghreb (*m*)	*North Africa*
s'expatrier	*to leave one's country*	mode (*m*) de vie	*way of life*
fixation (*f*)	*settling*	naturalisation (*f*)	*naturalisation*
flux (*m*) migratoire		pays (*m*) d'adoption	
	flood of immigrants		*adopted country*
foyer (*m*)	*hostel*	pays (*m*) d'origine	*country of origin*
ghetto (*m*)	*ghetto*	pays (*m*) natal	*country of birth*
Hexagone (*m*)	*France*	pièce (*f*) d'identité	*identity card*
inadapté/e	*not fitting in*	refouler	*to turn back, refuse entry*
insertion (*f*)	*integration*	résider	*to be resident*
s'installer	*to settle*	terre (*f*) d'accueil	*host country*
s'intégrer	*to fit in*	visa (*m*)	*visa*

renier leurs coutumes	*to give up their customs*
abuser de l'hospitalité	*to take unfair advantage of hospitality*
demander le droit d'asile	*to ask for political asylum*
bénéficier des droits sociaux	*to get social security*
être# en situation irrégulière	*to be breaking the law*
réglementer l'immigration	*to control immigration*
renier leurs racines	*to deny their roots*
le regroupement familial	*reuniting a family*
entrer en fraude	*to enter illegally*
obtenir# la nationalité française	*to become a French national*
surmonter des barrières linguistiques	*to overcome linguistic barriers*
le passage de la frontière	*crossing the border*
assimilé/e à la société française	*absorbed into French society*

LE RACISME

		extrême droite (*f*)	*far right*
		Front (*m*) national	*National Front*
antisémitisme (*m*)	anti-semitism	gêner quelqu'un	*to bother someone*
brute (*m*)	*bully*	grief (*m*)	*grievance*
émeute raciale (*f*)	*race riot*	haine (*f*)	*hatred*
enrayer	*to curb*	harcèlement (*m*) policier	
ethnie (*f*)	*ethnic group*		*police harassment*

inciter	*to stir up*
intensification (*f*)	*escalation*
intolérance (*f*)	*intolerance*
méfiance (*f*)	*distrust*
mobile (*m*)	*motive*
opprimer	*to oppress*
pagaille (*f*)	*chaos*
parti (*m*) fasciste	*Fascist party*
racisme (*m*)	*racism*
se radicaliser	*to intensify*
railler	*to taunt*

rancœur (*f*)	*resentment*
rapatrier	*to repatriate*
ratonnade (*f*)	*attack on immigrants*
rejeter#	*to reject*
relations (*fpl*) inter-raciales	*race relations*
violence (*f*) raciste	*racial violence*
voyou (*m*)	*hooligan*
xénophobie (*f*)	*hatred of foreigners*

avoir# des préjugés racistes	*to be racially prejudiced*
le seuil de tolérance	*the threshold of tolerance*
la commission chargée de supprimer la discrimination raciale	*race relations board*
attiser les passions	*to stir up feelings*
une attaque raciste	*racially-motivated attack*
le traitement préférentiel	*preferential treatment*
sa couleur joue contre lui	*his colour counts against him*
la recrudescence du racisme	*the upsurge in racism*
la montée de l'extrême droite	*the rise of the far right*
renvoyer# les immigrés chez eux	*to send immigrants back home*
la banalisation des idées racistes	*the commonplace acceptance of racist ideas*
désamorcer# la montée du racisme	*to counteract the increase in racism*
les idées lepénistes	*Le Pen's extreme right-wing ideas*
le respect de la dignité humaine	*respect for human dignity*
un nombre croissant d'agressions racistes	*a growing number of racist attacks*
juger selon la couleur de la peau	*to judge on the basis of the colour of someone's skin*
le racisme procède d'un écheveau de facteurs différents	*racism stems from a whole raft of different factors*
le racisme est l'un des défis majeurs auxquels est confrontée notre société	*racism is one of the major challenges facing our society*

DIVERS

binational/e	*holding dual nationality*
collectivité (*f*)	*the community*
diversité (*f*) culturelle	*cultural diversity*
droits (*mpl*) de l'homme	*human rights*
édifice (*m*) social	*social fabric*
expulser	*to expel*
idée (*f*) erronée	*false idea*
inassimilable	*unable to be assimilated*

laxisme (*m*)	*being too soft*
marginalisé/e	*edged out, ignored*
mariage (*m*) de convenance	*marriage of convenience*
mariage (*m*) forcé	*forced marriage*
mœurs (*fpl*) locales	*local customs*
multiracial/e	*multiracial*
ouvertement	*openly*
rapatriement (*m*)	*repatriation*
réprimer	*to crack down on*

améliorer les relations entre	*to improve relationships between*
à cheval entre deux sociétés	*to be split between two societies*
faire# un effort d'adaptation	*to try to adapt*
la patrie d'élection	*the country of one's own choosing*
de souche française	*of old French stock*
une famille étendue	*extended family*
d'après la rumeur publique	*according to popular belief*

SITES INTERNET UTILES

www.gbhr.eurorscg.fr/gbhr/campagnes/sos_racisme.html (site de SOS Racisme)

www.unhcr.ch/french/fwelcome.htm (haut commissariat des nations unies pour les réfugiés)

http://europa.eu.int/scadplus/leg/fr/cha/c10417.htm (plan d'action contre le racisme)

www.mrap.asso.fr (mouvement contre le racisme et pour l'amitié entre les peuples)

www.licra.com (Ligue internationale contre le racisme et l'antisémitisme)

www.front-nat.fr (site du Front National)

www.francealacarte.org.uk (le site du réseau culturel français au Royaume-Uni)

www.admifrance.gouv.fr (un annuaire des sites Internet français)

LA FRANCE

UNE RÉGION DE FRANCE

accidenté/e	hilly
accueil (m)	welcome
arriéré/e	backward
arrière-pays (m)	hinterland
aspect (m) touristique	touristy side
atmosphère (f)	atmosphere
cadre (m) de vie	living environment
caractéristique (f)	characteristic
carnaval (m)	carnival
climat (m)	climate
commémorer	to commemorate
se concentrer	to be concentrated
connu/e	well-known
contraste (m)	contrast
cultivable	suitable for growing
démuni/e	deprived
dépendant/e de	dependent on
développement (m)	development
doté/e de	endowed with
dynamisme (m)	dynamism
économie (f) diversifiée	varied economy
économie (f) régionale	regional economy
s'enorgueillir de	to pride itself on
ensoleillement (m)	hours of sunshine

essor (m)	expansion
facteur (m)	factor
faiblesse (f)	weakness
fier/ière de	proud of
florissant/e	flourishing
forestier/ière	forest (adj)
habitat (m)	habitat
image (f) de marque	public image
industrie (f) de pointe	high-tech industry
kermesse (f)	fair
littoral (m)	shore, coast
médiéval/e	medieval
mélange (m)	mixture
méridional/e	southern
Midi (m)	South of France
patrimoine (m)	heritage
paysage (m)	countryside
peuplé/e	populated
pluviosité (f)	average rainfall
se promouvoir#	to promote itself
prospérité (f)	wealth
région (f) à problème	problem area
relief (m)	contours, relief
renommé/e pour	famous for
reprise (f)	recovery, revival
richesses (fpl)	riches, wealth
secteur (m) tertiaire	service industries

sophistiqué/e	*sophisticated*
spécificité (*f*)	*distinctive feature*
témoigner de	*to indicate, bear witness to*
traditionnel/le	*traditional*
typique	*typical*
se vanter de	*to boast, be proud of*

vestiges (*mpl*) historiques	*historical remains*
ville (*f*) universitaire	*university town*
vitalité (*f*)	*vitality*
viticole	*wine-growing*

garder son identité unique	*to keep its unique identity*
sa situation géographique privilégiée	*its favoured geographical position*
la flore et la faune	*the plant and animal life*
une province à vocation agricole	*an agricultural province*
les particularismes régionaux	*regional idiosyncracies*
la douceur de son climat	*the mildness of its climate*
la disparition des industries traditionnelles	*the disappearance of traditional industries*
dépasser la moyenne nationale	*to be above the national average*
refléter# la puissance passée de	*to mirror the former power of*
disposer d'atouts considérables	*to have some considerable advantages*
attirer des entreprises	*to attract businesses*
c'est une région durement touchée par	*it's an area badly affected by*
vivre# une profonde mutation	*to undergo profound changes*
un site naturel	*an area of outstanding natural beauty*
la région bénéficie de	*the area benefits from*
une région à faible densité de population	*a sparsely populated area*

LA RÉSISTANCE

Allemagne (*f*) nazie	*Nazi Germany*
alliés (*mpl*)	*the Allies*
appareil (*m*) policier	*police machinery*
apport (*m*)	*contribution*
armée (*f*) des ombres	*secret army*

armée (*f*) occupante	*army of occupation*
armée (*f*) souterraine	*underground army*
armistice (*m*)	*armistice*
arrestation (*f*)	*arrest*
attentat (*m*)	*attack*

attentisme (*m*)	*wait and see policy*
balisage (*m*)	*marking out*
belligérant (*m*)	*nation at war*
camp (*m*) de concentration	*concentration camp*
capitulation (*f*)	*surrender*
cesser le combat	*to stop fighting*
clandestin/e	*secret*
clandestinité (*f*)	*resistance*
collaborateur/trice (*m/f*)	*collaborator*
collaboration (*f*)	*collaboration*
combattant/e (*m/f*)	*combatant*
coordonner	*to co-ordinate*
couvre-feu (*m*)	*curfew*
croix (*f*) gammée	*swastika*
défaite (*f*)	*defeat*
délivrer la France	*to set France free*
démoralisation (*f*)	*demoralisation*
dénonciation (*f*)	*exposure, betrayal*
déportation (*f*)	*internment, imprisonment in a concentration camp*
déporté/e (*m/f*)	*internee, person sent to a concentration camp*
détachement (*m*)	*detachment*
diffuser	*to spread, distribute*
dirigeant /e (*m/f*)	*leader*
drôle (*m*) de guerre	*phoney war*
en exil (*m*)	*in exile*
encercler	*to surround*
envahisseur (*m*)	*invader*
s'évader	*to escape*
faux papiers (*mpl*)	*forged papers*
forces (*fpl*) allemandes	*German forces*
franc-tireur (*m*)	*irregular soldier*
fusiller	*to shoot*
guerre-éclair (*f*)	*'blitzkrieg', lightning war*
harcèlement (*m*)	*harrying*
harceler	*to harry*
îlot (*m*) de résistance	*pocket of resistance*
s'implanter	*to establish itself*
interpellation (*f*)	*detention for questioning*
interrogation (*f*)	*questioning*
jour (*m*) J	*D-day*
libérateur (*m*)	*liberator*
libération (*f*)	*liberation*
ligne (*f*) de démarcation	*demarcation line*
loyauté (*f*)	*loyalty*
maquis (*m*)	*the Resistance*
maquisard (*m*)	*member of the Resistance*
maréchal (*m*)	*marshal*
massacrer	*to massacre*
milice (*f*)	*militia*
mobilisation (*f*)	*mobilisation*
mouvement (*m*)	*movement*
narguer	*to flout*
otage (*m*)	*hostage*
papillon (*m*)	*sticker, bill*
parachuter	*to parachute*
paralyser	*to paralyse*
patriote (*m/f*)	*patriot*
pays (*m*) allié	*allied country*

percée (*f*)	*breakthrough*	renforcement (*m*)	*reinforcement*
piller	*to pillage*	représailles (*fpl*)	*reprisals*
poignée (*f*) d'hommes		réseau (*m*) d'évasion	
	handful of men		*escape network*
population (*f*) civile		résistant/e (*m/f*)	*resistance fighter*
	civilian population	revers (*m*)	*setback*
presse (*f*) clandestine		riposte (*f*)	*counter-attack*
	underground press	sabotage (*m*)	*sabotage*
prisonnier (*m*) de guerre		saboter	*to sabotage*
	prisoner of war	sévices (*mpl*)	*ill treatment*
privations (*fpl*)	*hardship*	sol (*m*) français	*French soil*
rafle (*f*)	*round-up*	tournant (*m*)	*turning point*
rallier	*to unite*	tract (*m*)	*pamphlet*
rassembler	*to round up*	trahison (*f*)	*betrayal*
rationnement (*m*)	*rationing*	traître (*m*)	*traitor*
ravager#	*to lay waste*	traquer	*to track down*
ravitaillement (*m*)	*resupplying*	troupes (*fpl*)	*troops*
recrue (*f*)	*recruit*	vainqueur (*m*)	*victor*
réfractaire (*m*)	*draft dodger*	zone (*f*) occupée	*occupied zone*
régime (*m*) de Vichy	*the Vichy régime*		

exercer# des représailles contre	*to carry out reprisals against*
malgré des revers et des pertes considérables	*despite setbacks and heavy losses*
Moulin fut brutalisé par ses tortionnaires	*Moulin was brutally treated by his torturers*
porter un coup à la machine de guerre nazie	*to deal a blow to the nazi war machine*
prendre# l'ennemi à revers	*to attack the enemy from behind*
les autorités vichyssoises	*the Vichy authorities*
des attaques contre des objectifs allemands	*attacks on German targets*
le bilan total des morts est inconnu	*the death toll is unknown*
le rôle de la presse clandestine	*the role of the underground press*

la guerre psychologique	*the psychological war*
mourir# pour la patrie	*to die for one's country*
faire# un coup d'éclat	*to create a commotion*
faire# quelque chose en cachette	*to do something secretly*
la propagande de guerre	*war propaganda*

LA FRANCOPHONIE

abâtardi/e	*bastardised*
accent (*m*)	*accent*
amalgame (*m*)	*mixture*
analphabète	*illiterate*
s'angliciser	*to become anglicised*
anglophone	*English-speaking*
autochtone	*native*
autonomie (*f*)	*self-determination*
bilingue	*bilingual*
bilinguisme (*m*)	*bilingualism*
chauvin/e	*chauvinistic*
coexistence (*f*)	*co-existence*
colonisation (*f*)	*colonisation*
Créole (*m*)	*Creole language*
de souche latine	*of Latin origin*
décolonisation (*f*)	*decolonisation*
enraciné/e	*deep-rooted*
évoluer	*to evolve*
ex-colonies (*fpl*)	*former colonies*
s'exprimer	*to express oneself*
francophile (*m/f*)	*lover of France*
francophone	*French-speaking*
franglais (*m*)	*French/English mix*
hégémonie (*f*) culturelle	*cultural domination*
s'imposer	*to dominate*
langue (*f*) administrative	*administrative language*
langue (*f*) maternelle	*mother tongue*
langue (*f*) officielle	*official language*
langue (*f*) véhiculaire	*common language*
lien (*m*) historique	*historic link*
Métropole (*f*)	*France*
orbite (*f*) française	*French sphere of influence*
parlant (*m*) français	*French speaker*
patois (*m*)	*dialect*
périphrase (*f*)	*circumlocution*
pied-noir (*m*)	*Algerian-born French person*
puriste (*m/f*)	*purist*
rayonner	*to extend*
ressortissant/e (*m/f*)	*national*
supplanter	*to take the place of*

soumis/e à l'influence française	*under French influence*
avoir# quelque chose en commun avec	*to have something in common with*
le français du Québec a des spécificités	*Canadian French has some idiosyncracies*

41

des liens privilégiés avec le Maghreb	*preferential ties with North Africa*
les notices sont rédigées en deux langues	*notices are drawn up in two languages*
le français est le véhicule de communication commun	*French is the common language for conversation*
les anciennes colonies françaises et belges	*former French and Belgian colonies*
les DOM-TOM (Départements et territoires d'Outre-Mer)	*French overseas administrative regions and territories*
un journal d'expression française	*a French-language newspaper*
un sabir fait de français et d'arabe	*a mixture of French and Arabic*
l'apprentissage du français	*learning French*
des cours d'alphabétisation	*literacy lessons*
le français coexiste parallèlement à la langue locale	*French coexists alongside the local language*

LA POLITIQUE

abstentionnisme (*m*)	*abstaining*
affaires (*fpl*) étrangères	*foreign affairs*
aller# aux urnes	*to go to the polls*
alternance (*f*)	*handing over of power*
bourgeois/e	*middle-class*
briguer	*to canvass*
bureau (*m*) de vote	*polling station*
campagne (*f*)	*campaign*
chef (*m*) d'État	*head of state*
circonscription (*f*)	*constituency*
citoyenneté (*f*)	*citizenship*
civisme (*m*)	*public-spiritedness*
cohabiter	*to work together*
corrompu/e	*corrupt*
décideurs (*mpl*)	*decision-makers*
décréter#	*to order, decree*
délégué/e (*m/f*)	*delegate*

démentir#	*to deny*
démission (*f*)	*resignation*
député (*m*)	*MP*
désaccord (*m*)	*disagreement*
dictature (*f*)	*dictatorship*
discours (*m*)	*speech*
électeur/trice (*m/f*)	*constituent*
élection (*f*) cantonale	*local election*
élection (*f*) municipale	*municipal election*
élection (*f*) partielle	*by-election*
élections (*fpl*) présidentielles	*presidential elections*
électorat (*m*)	*electorate*
élire#	*to elect*
élus (*mpl*)	*elected members*
engagement (*m*)	*commitment*
entretiens (*mpl*)	*talks*
gauchiste (*m*)	*left-winger*

homologue (*m*)
    counterpart, opposite number

indépendantiste (*m/f*)
    freedom fighter

inégalités (*fpl*) sociales
    social inequalities

jour (*m*) des élections   *polling day*

légiférer#   *to legislate*

majoritaire   *in the majority*

manifester   *to demonstrate*

membre (*m*) de la droite
    right-winger

mondialisation (*f*)   *globalisation*

opposant (*m*)   *opponent*

parlementaire (*m/f*)   *MP*

partage (*m*) du pouvoir
    power sharing

parti (*m*) au pouvoir   *party in office*

parti (*m*) conservateur
    Conservative party (UK)

parti (*m*) d'extrême droite
    far right party

parti (*m*) travailliste
    Labour party (UK)

politique (*f*)   *politics, policy*

politisé/e   *politically aware*

porte-parole (*m*)   *spokesperson*

pouvoir (*m*)   *power*

pouvoirs (*mpl*)   *public authorities*

préfet (*m*)
    prefect (local government)

premier ministre (*m*)   *prime minister*

prolétaire   *working-class*

promesse (*f*)   *promise*

proportionnelle (*f*)
    proportional representation

quinquennat (*m*)
    five year term of office

référendum (*m*)   *referendum*

scandale (*f*)   *scandal*

score (*m*)   *result*

scrutin (*m*)   *ballot*

septennat (*m*)
    seven-year term of office

siéger#   *to sit*

sommet (*m*)   *summit*

sondage (*m*)   *opinion poll*

suffrage (*m*) universel   *votes for all*

valise (*f*) diplomatique
    diplomatic bag

voix (*f*)   *vote*

voter massivement
    to vote overwhelmingly

---

la participation aux scrutins électoraux   *turnout at the polls*

lancer# un appel au gouvernement   *to appeal to the government*

suivre# des démarches pour   *to take steps to*

il incombe au gouvernement d'agir   *it's up to the government to act*

le scrutin majoritaire   *first past the post system*

politiquement correct   *politically correct*

faire# reculer les inégalités sociales	*to reduce unfairness in society*
sur le plan politique	*on a political level*
conserver son siège	*to keep his/her seat*
préconiser des mesures à long terme	*to be in favour of long-term measures*
se faire# plébisciter	*to gain a landslide victory*
la chute du communisme	*the fall of communism*
le conseil régional	*county council*
adhérer à un parti politique	*to belong to a political party*
avoir# la cote auprès des Français	*to be very popular with the French*
remporter les élections	*to win the election*
les courants de l'opinion	*trends of public opinion*
la politique agricole commune	*common agricultural policy*
la fragilisation des systèmes politiques	*the weakening of political systems*
se méfier des politiciens	*to distrust politicians*

LA GASTRONOMIE

alimentation (*f*) de base	*staple diet*
alimenter	*to nourish*
aliments (*mpl*) complets	*wholefoods*
appétit (*m*)	*appetite*
aromate (*m*)	*herb, spice*
aromatiser	*to flavour*
arôme (*m*)	*aroma*
artisanal/e	*locally produced*
assaisonnement (*m*)	*seasoning, dressing*
bénéfique	*beneficial*
bouchée (*f*)	*mouthful*
calorie (*f*)	*calorie*
cholestérol (*m*)	*cholesterol*
en conserve	*tinned, canned*

conserves (*fpl*)	*tinned foods*
consommateur/trice (*m/f*)	*customer*
consommation (*f*)	*consumption, drink*
consommer	*to eat, consume*
couvert (*m*)	*place setting*
crustacés (*mpl*)	*shellfish*
cuisine (*f*) du terroir	*local cooking*
cuisine (*f*) minceur	*lean cuisine*
culinaire	*culinary*
dégustation (*f*)	*tasting*
délice (*m*)	*delight*
désaltérer#	*to quench thirst*
épicé/e	*spicy*
féculents (*mpl*)	*starchy foods*
friandise (*f*)	*delicacy*

gastronome (*m/f*)	*gourmet*
gastronomique	*gourmet*
gorgée (*f*)	*mouthful*
goûteux/euse	*tasty*
haute cuisine (*f*)	*top-class cooking*
ingrédient (*m*)	*ingredient*
laitages (*mpl*)	*milk products*
matière (*f*) grasse	*fat content*
millésime (*m*)	*vintage*
mousseux/euse	*sparkling*
odorat (*m*)	*sense of smell*
œnologie (*f*)	*science of winemaking*
pièce (*f*) de résistance	*main dish*
plat (*m*) de résistance	*main dish of the meal*
plat (*m*) du jour	*today's special*
plateau (*m*) de fromages	*cheese board*
plats (*mpl*) cuisinés	*ready-cooked dishes*

priser	*to prize, appreciate*
produit (*m*) laitier	*dairy product*
recette (*f*)	*recipe*
rendement (*m*)	*yield*
repas (*m*) d'affaires	*business lunch*
restaurant (*m*) diététique	*health-food restaurant*
restaurant (*m*) gastronomique	*gourmet restaurant*
restaurateur (*m*)	*restaurant owner*
récolte (*f*)	*harvest*
savoureux/euse	*tasty*
sous-vide	*vacuum-packed*
se suralimenter	*to overeat*
transgénique	*genetically modified*
valeur (*f*) nutritive	*nutritional value*
végétarien/ne	*vegetarian*
vignoble (*m*)	*vineyard*
vitamine (*f*)	*vitamin*

le savoir vivre	*an appreciation of how to live well*
la restauration rapide	*fast-food industry*
avoir# une prédilection pour	*to be partial to*
privilégier la cuisine traditionnelle	*to prefer traditional cooking*
l'équipement électroménager	*domestic appliances*
les plats préparés surgelés	*ready-made frozen foods*
l'appétit vient en mangeant	*eating whets your appetite*
aimer les plaisirs de la table	*to like one's food*
quelle est la composition du gâteau?	*what's the cake made of?*
c'est le seul art qui parle aux cinq sens	*it's the only art that appeals to all five senses*
faire# un écart gastronomique	*to eat out*

la valeur nutritive	*nutritional value*
des produits garantis sans OGM	*no genetically modified ingredients*
avoir# une alimentation équilibrée	*to eat a balanced diet*

SITES INTERNET UTILES

www.urec.cnrs.fr/annuaire (annuaire sur les régions de la France)

http://Club.ovh.net/pyrenees (site des Pyrénées)

www.bretagne.com (le magazine de la Bretagne)

www.multimania.com/h2gm/mresistance.html (site sur la résistance)

http://perso.infonie.fr/grandalf (association des amis du musée de la résistance)

www.ina.fr/Archives/Guerre/index.light.fr.html (archives sur la deuxième guerre mondiale)

www.francophonie.org (l'organisation internationale de la Francophonie)

www.adomonde.qc.ca (site pour les adolescents de la Francophonie)

www.departments.bucknell.edu/french/internet/francophonie/index.html (la page de la Francophonie)

www.assemblee-nationale.fr (site de l'Assemblée Nationale)

www.assemblee-nationale.fr/1/mondial (le parlement des enfants)

www.france.diplomatie.fr/france/index.html (site de la France Diplomatie)

www.francealacarte.org.uk (le site du réseau culturel français au Royaume-Uni)

www.diplomatie.gouv.fr (des infos sur la politique)

www.ambafrance.org/LINKS/ (site sur la gourmandise)

www.europe-gastronomie.fr (site de l'Agence Agro-Alimentaire)

LES GENS

LA FAMILLE

adoptif/ve	*adopted*
adultère (*m*)	*adultery*
agence (*f*) matrimoniale	*dating agency*
allocation (*f*) familiale	*child benefit*
cellule (*f*) familiale	*family unit*
concubinage (*m*)	*common-law marriage*
conflit (*m*) conjugal	*marital strife*
conjoint/e (*m/f*)	*spouse*
démuni/e	*deprived*
se désagréger#	*to break up*
divorcer	*to divorce*
épouser	*to get married*
esprit (*m*) de famille	*family feeling*
famille (*f*) adoptive	*foster home*
famille (*f*) monoparentale	*single-parent family*
famille (*f*) nombreuse	*large family*
famille (*f*) nucléaire	*nuclear family*
femme (*f*) battue	*battered wife*
fonder un foyer (*m*)	*to set up a home*
foyer (*m*) brisé	*broken home*
homme (*m*) au foyer	*house husband*
liens (*m*) familiaux	*family ties*
mariage (*m*)	*marriage*
se marier	*to get married*
ménagère (*f*)	*housewife*
mère (*f*) d'accueil	*surrogate mother*
mère (*f*) célibataire	*single mother*
mœurs (*fpl*)	*morals*
monogame	*monogamous*
natalité (*f*)	*birth rate*
nid (*m*) douillet	*cosy nest*
parent (*m*) isolé	*single parent*
partenaire (*m/f*)	*partner*
planning (*m*) familial	*family planning*
structure (*f*) familiale	*family structure*
s'unir	*to be joined in marriage*
veuf/veuve (*m/f*)	*widower/widow*
vie (*f*) en couple	*life together*

contrat m de mariage	*marriage contract*
se mettre# en ménage	*to set up house together*
vivre# en union libre	*to live together*
se solder par un divorce	*to end in divorce*
la garde des enfants	*custody of the children*
le taux de nuptialité est en baisse	*the marriage rate is in decline*

vivre# en dehors du cadre de mariage	*to live outside the framework of marriage*
les naissances hors mariage	*births outside marriage*
le vieillissement de la population	*the aging population*
une famille éclatée	*extended family*
un couple non-marié	*an unmarried couple*
le taux de fécondité	*the birth-rate*
vivre# en solo	*to stay single*
vivre# séparé	*to live apart*
tenir# compte du milieu familial	*to take the family background into account*

LE CONFLIT DES GÉNÉRATIONS

agaçant/e	*annoying*
autoritaire	*authoritarian*
bouder	*to sulk*
comportement (*m*)	*behaviour*
se comporter	*to behave*
confiance (*f*)	*confidence*
contredire#	*to contradict*
coup (*m*) de cafard	*fit of depression*
crise (*f*)	*crisis*
culture (*f*) adolescente	*teenage culture*
délaisser	*to neglect*
dépassé/e	*old-fashioned*
désaccord (*m*)	*disagreement*
désobéir à quelqu'un	*to disobey someone*

dialoguer avec	*to communicate with*
dispute (*f*)	*argument*
droits (*mpl*) des enfants	*children's rights*
environnement (*m*) stable	*stable environment*
échelle (*f*) des valeurs	*scale of values*
élever	*to rear, raise*
étouffant/e	*suffocating*
excès (*m*) d'autorité	*over-strictness*
faire# une fugue	*to run away*
fermeté (*f*)	*firmness*
frictions (*f*) parents-enfants	*parent-child conflicts*
hostilité (*f*)	*hostility*
incompréhension (*f*)	*lack of understanding*
indulgent/e	*lenient*
liens (*mpl*) familiaux	*family ties*
lubie (*f*)	*whim, fad*

marginal (*m*)	*drop-out*
mauvais traitement (*m*) d'enfants	
	child abuse
mépriser	*to scorn*
mûr/e	*mature*
s'occuper des enfants	
	to look after the children
ouvert/e	*open*
piercing (*m*)	*body piercing*
progéniture (*f*)	*offspring*
protecteur/trice à l'excès	
	over-protective
puberté (*f*)	*puberty*
rapports (*mpl*)	*relationships*
rebelle (*m/f*)	*rebel*
se rebeller contre	*to rebel against*

rechigner	*to look sour*
reproche (*m*)	*criticism*
respecter	*to respect*
se révolter	*to rebel*
sentiment (*m*)	*feeling*
se sentir# brimé/e	*to feel got at*
se sentir# incompris/e	
	to feel misunderstood
sévère	*strict*
soucis (*m*)	*care, worry*
soutenir#	*to support*
surprotéger#	*to overprotect*
traiter	*to treat*
uni/e	*united*
valeurs (*fpl*) familiales	*family values*

les jeunes désœuvrés	*young people with nothing to do*
rompre avec son enfance	*to break with one's childhood*
être# ballotté/e entre des sentiments contradictoires	*to be torn between conflicting emotions*
la transmission des valeurs traditionnelles	*the passing on of traditional values*
accorder de l'autonomie à	*to grant someone their independence*
manquer de respect envers	*to lack respect for*
s'enfermer dans la chambre	*to shut oneself away in the bedroom*
mener# à l'harmonie familiale	*to make for family harmony*
être# replié/e sur soi-même	*to be inward-looking*
imposer leur volonté	*to impose their will*
mes parents dramatisent trop	*my parents over-react*
avoir# des rapports tendus avec	*to have a strained relationship with*
être# traité/e différemment de	*to be treated differently to*
les parents sont responsables de	*parents are responsible for*
quitter le foyer familial	*to leave home*

ils n'arrêtent pas de faire des remarques	*they're always nagging*
saper l'autorité parentale	*to undermine parental authority*
l'organisation 'Allô! Enfance maltraitée'	*French equivalent to Childline*
je dois supporter beaucoup de choses	*I have to put up with a lot*
privé/e d'affection	*emotionally deprived*

L'AMOUR ET L'AMITIÉ

âge (*m*) de consentement sexuel	*age of consent*
amoureux/euse de	*in love with*
attirance (*f*)	*attraction*
s'amuser	*to have fun*
bouleverser	*to upset deeply*
chagrin (*m*) d'amour	*boyfriend/girlfriend problem*
cohabitation (*f*)	*living together*
cohabiter	*to live together*
confiance (*f*)	*confidence*
défaut (*m*)	*failing, fault*
déranger	*to upset*
se disputer avec	*to quarrel with*
enceinte	*pregnant*
énerver	*to irritate*
s'entendre bien avec	*to get on well with*
fréquenter	*to go around with*

gêné/e	*embarrassed*
intimité (*f*)	*intimacy*
offenser quelqu'un	*to hurt somebody's feelings*
s'opposer à	*to be against*
partager	*to share*
plaquer	*to dump, ditch*
pression (*f*)	*pressure*
rapports (*mpl*) sexuels	*sexual intercourse*
se réconcilier avec	*to make up with*
respecter	*to respect*
rigoler	*to have a laugh*
romantisme (*m*)	*romanticism*
sensé/e	*sensible*
sensible	*sensitive*
sortir# avec	*to go out with*
tendresse (*f*)	*affection*
traîner avec	*to hang around with*
vie (*f*) amoureuse	*love life*
vie (*f*) affective	*emotional life*

faire# la tête à quelqu'un	*to sulk with somebody*
avoir# confiance en quelqu'un	*to trust somebody*
tomber amoureux/se de	*to fall in love with*
garder le moral	*to keep your spirits up*
emménager ensemble	*to move in together*

se mettre en ménage avec	*to set up house with*
le mari idéal	*Mister Right*
s'investir dans une relation	*to put a lot into a relationship*
manquer d'égards envers	*to be inconsiderate towards*

LES DROITS ET LES RESPONSABILITÉS

citoyen/ne (*m/f*)	*citizen*
devenir# adulte	*to grow up*
devoir (*m*)	*duty*
droit (*m*) de vote	*the right to vote*
droits (*mpl*)	*rights*
jeux (*mpl*) d'argent	*gambling*
majeur/e	*over 18*
maturité (*f*)	*maturity*
mineur/e	*under 18*
morale (*f*)	*morality*

mûr/e	*mature*
mûrir	*to mature*
nombriliste	*self-centred*
parier	*to bet*
permis (*m*) de conduire	*driving licence*
puéril/e	*childish*
répercussion (*f*)	*implication*
responsabilité (*f*)	*responsibility*
serviable	*willing to help*
service (*m*) militaire	*national service*
tuteur (*m*) légal	*legal guardian*

avoir# le droit de faire quelque chose	*to be entitled to do something*
être# en âge de	*to be old enough to*
responsabiliser quelqu'un	*to make somebody aware of their responsibilities*
le sens du devoir	*the sense of duty*
avoir# le sens civique	*to have a sense of civic responsibility*
assumer ses responsabilités	*to take on one's responsibilities*
réussir sa vie	*to succeed in life*
la liberté individuelle	*personal freedom*
atteindre# sa majorité	*to come of age*
l'autorisation parentale	*parental consent*
responsable aux yeux de la loi	*legally responsible*
être# responsable de ses actes	*to be responsible for one's actions*
les actes ont des conséquences	*actions have consequences*
agir à la légère	*to act irresponsibly*
acheter un billet de loterie	*to buy a lottery ticket*

LE RÔLE DE LA FEMME

abaisser	to humiliate
ambitieux/euse	ambitious
améliorer	to improve
autonome	self-sufficient
carrière (f)	career
condition (f) féminine	woman's lot
contradictoire	contradictory
se culpabiliser	to feel guilty
se débrouiller	to cope
désapprouver quelque chose	to disapprove of something
discrimination (f) sexuelle	sexual discrimination
droits (mpl) de la femme	women's rights
égalitaire	egalitarian
égalité (f) des chances	equality of opportunity
égalité (f) des sexes	equality of the sexes
émancipation (f)	emancipation
émancipé/e	liberated
s'épanouir	to be fulfilled
grief (m)	grievance
groupe (m) féministe	women's group
harcèlement (m) sexuel	sexual harassment
idéaliser	to idealise
interdit (m)	taboo
libération (f) de la femme	women's liberation
liberté (f)	freedom
machiste	male chauvinist
mal vu/e	poorly thought of
maternel/le	motherly
maternité (f)	motherhood
mère (f) célibataire	unmarried mother
militantisme (m)	militancy
misogynie (f)	misogyny
mouvement (m) féministe	feminist movement
moyens (mpl) financiers	financial means
objet (m) érotique	sex object
parité (f)	equality
phallocrate (m)	male chauvinist
pionnière (f)	pioneer
préjugé (m)	prejudice
pressions (fpl) sociales	social pressures
réclamer	to demand
répartition (f) des rôles	division of the roles
rester au foyer	to stay at home
sexe (m) opposé	opposite sex
sexisme (m)	sexism
stéréotype (m)	stereotype
subir	to be subjected to
surmonter	to overcome

à travail égal, salaire égal	*equal pay for equal work*
être# conditionné/e à	*to be conditioned to*
s'intéresser avant tout à sa carrière	*to be a career person*
le partage des tâches ménagères	*sharing the household jobs*
l'avortement sur demande	*abortion on demand*
la moitié de la race humaine	*half of the human race*
accéder# à la vie professionnelle	*to have access to a career*
conserver son nom de jeune fille	*to keep her maiden name*
être# déterminée par sa fonction de procréation	*to be bound by their reproductive function*
démythifier la maternité	*to remove the myths about motherhood*
rémunérer les femmes au foyer	*to pay housewives for their work*
se sentir# prisonnier/ière	*to feel trapped*
servir# de modèle à émuler	*to act as a role model*
concilier travail et famille	*to juggle work and a family*

LES GENS CÉLÈBRES

admirer	*to admire*
anonymat (*m*)	*anonymity*
bain (*m*) de foule	*walkabout*
blasé/e	*laid-back*
célébrité (*f*)	*fame*
culte (*m*) du héros	*hero-worship*
de renommée mondiale	*world-famous*
devoir (*m*)	*duty*
doué/e	*talented*
dynastie (*f*)	*dynasty*
extravagant/e	*flamboyant*
héritier (*m*) de la couronne	*heir apparent*
hors d'atteinte	*beyond reach*
s'identifier à	*to identify with*
idolâtrer	*to idolise*
impressionnant/e	*impressive*
inaugurer	*to unveil, open*
influencer#	*to influence*
luxe (*m*)	*luxury*
millionnaire (*m/f*)	*millionaire*
mode (*m*) de vie	*life-style*
monarchie (*f*)	*monarchy*
notoire	*notorious*
personnalité (*f*)	*famous person*
popularité (*f*)	*popularity*
privilégié/e	*privileged*
régner#	*to reign*
reine (*f*)	*queen*
remarquable	*remarkable*
renommé/e pour	*renowned for, famous for*

richesse (*f*)	*wealth*	souverain/e (*m/f*)	*sovereign*
roi (*m*)	*king*	vedette (*f*)	*star*
snobisme (*m*)	*snobbery*	vivats (*mpl*)	*cheers*

une légende de son vivant	*a legend in his/her own lifetime*
mener# une vie intolérable	*to lead an unbearable life*
présider une cérémonie	*to be guest of honour at a ceremony*
la famille royale britannique	*the British royal family*
exercer une fascination sur	*to exert a fascination over*
rendre# hommage à	*to pay tribute to*
très populaire auprès des jeunes	*very popular amongst young people*
il ne peut pas passer inaperçu	*he cannot go unrecognised*

SITES INTERNET UTILES

http://globegate.utm.edu/french/globegate_mirror/famille.html (site sur la famille)

www.admifrance.gouv.fr (un annuaire des sites Internet français)

www.pratique.fr/vieprat/fam/ (tout sur la famille)

www.class.csupomona.edu/efl/french308/famille_moderne.html (la famille française moderne)

www.access.ch/logma/afg/gtff.htm (femme, famille et société)

www.oritech.com/voixdelles (association féministe française)

http://perso.wanadoo.fr/ev/FMCP/ (fédération des mouvements de la condition paternelle)

www.bruxelles-j.be/index.htm (site d'information jeunesse)

www.information-jeunesse.tm.fr/ (centre d'information et de documentation jeunesse)

LA SCIENCE ET LA TECHNOLOGIE

LA TECHNOLOGIE

s'adapter	*to adapt*
apesanteur (*m*)	*weightlessness*
fusée (*f*)	*rocket*
génétique (*f*)	*genetics*
navette (*f*) spatiale	*space shuttle*

pointeur (*m*) laser	*laser pen*
spationaute (*mf*)	*astronaut*
station (*f*) spatiale	*space station*
téléguider	*to remote control*
téléphone (*m*) portable	*mobile phone*
transgénique	*genetically modified*

mettre# un satellite en orbite	*to put a satellite into orbit*
une sortie dans l'espace	*a space walk*
effectuer des expériences	*to carry out experiments*
les progrès scientifiques	*scientific advances*
les communications par satellites	*satellite communications*

LES ORDINATEURS

accro (*m*) du web	*web addict*
annuaire (*m*)	*directory*
base (*f*) de données	*database*
brancher	*to connect up*
bug (*m*) informatique	*virus*
CD-ROM (*m*)	*CD-Rom*
clavier (*m*)	*keyboard*
clavier tactile (*m*)	*concept keyboard*
cliquer sur	*to click on*
code (*m*) d'accès	*password*
compatible	*compatible*
convivial/e	*user-friendly*

copie (*f*) pirate	*pirate copy*
cybercafé (*m*)	*cybercafe*
cyberveuve (*f*)	*web widow*
disque (*m*) dur	*hard disk*
disquette (*f*)	*floppy disk*
écran (*m*)	*screen*
effraction (*f*) informatique	*hacking*
facture (*f*) téléphonique	*phone bill*
fiable	*reliable*
fichier (*m*)	*file*
forum (*m*) de discussion	*chat room*
fournisseur (*m*) d'accès	*Internet Service Provider*
frustrant/e	*frustrating*

imprimante (*f*)	*printer*
infographie (*f*)	*computer graphics*
informatiser	*to computerise*
internaute (*mf*)	*surfer*
jargon (*m*) informatique	*computerese*
jeu (*m*) électronique	*computer game*
en ligne	*on line*
listage (*m*)	*printout*
logiciel (*m*)	*software*
machine (*f*) de traitement de texte	*word processor*
matériel (*m*)	*hardware*
messagerie (*f*) électronique	*e-mail*
messageries (*fpl*) électroniques	*electronic bulletin board*
médiathèque (*f*)	*multi-media reference library*
mémoire (*f*)	*memory*
Minitel (*m*)	*home telecommunications terminal*
minitéliste (*m/f*)	*Minitel user*
mot (*m*) de passe	*password*

moteur (*m*) de recherche	*search engine*
ordinateur (*m*) individuel	*PC*
pirate (*m*) informatique	*hacker*
portable (*m*)	*laptop*
portatif/ve	*portable*
progiciel (*m*)	*software package*
puce (*f*)	*microchip*
réalité (*f*) virtuelle	*virtual reality*
réseau (*m*)	*network*
réseau (*m*) mondial	*World Wide Web*
sécuriser	*to make secure*
service (*m*) bancaire	*banking service*
site (*m*) Internet	*website*
souris (*f*)	*mouse*
terminal (*m*)	*terminal*
tomber en panne	*to crash*
touche (*f*)	*key*
traitement (*m*) graphique	*graphics*
usage (*m*) du web	*use of the internet*
utilisateur/trice (*m/f*)	*user*
virus (*m*)	*virus*

l'ère de l'informatique	*the computer age*
la sécurité des informations	*data security*
la loi informatique et libertés	*data protection act*
la qualité d'entrée égale la qualité de sortie	*garbage in, garbage out*
traiter quelque chose informatiquement	*to process something on a computer*
entrer dans le système	*to log on*
sortir# du système	*to log off*

dialoguer en direct avec	*to interact directly with*
Le Minitel est une spécificité française	*Minitel is unique to France*
faire# les courses par l'intermédiaire du Minitel	*to shop using Minitel*
initié/e à l'informatique	*computer literate*
l'enseignement assisté par ordinateur	*computer-assisted learning*
protéger les données personnelles	*to protect personal data*
être# connecté/e à Internet	*to be on the internet*
se servir# d'un ordinateur	*to use a computer*
un site très fréquenté	*a site that gets lots of hits*
facile à utiliser	*user-friendly*
pirater un réseau informatique	*to hack into a computer network*
tout va se faire sur ordinateur	*everything will be done by computer*
se promener sur Internet	*to surf the net*
la révolution informatique	*the information revolution*

SITES INTERNET UTILES

www.cnes.fr (centre national d'études spatiales)

www.bdl.fr/webastro.html (l'astronomie sur le web)

www.cite-sciences.fr/ (cite des sciences et de l'industrie)

www.admifrance.gouv.fr (un annuaire des sites Internet français)

www.sciencepresse.qc.ca/ (site pour les amis de Franco-science)

www.planet.fr/ (internet sans limite)

www.club-internet.fr (infos sur les sciences et l'informatique)

http://fr.dir.yahoo.com/Informatique_et_multimedia (des sites sur l'informatique)

http://perso.wanadoo.fr/olivier-c/AnnuaireWeb.html (la science et l'informatique)

LES MÉDIAS

LA TÉLÉVISION

actualité (f) scénarisée
'faction', drama documentary

allumer — to switch on

annonce (f) — announcement

antenne (f) parabolique
satellite dish

caméra (f) — video camera

canal (m) — channel

censurer — to censor

chaîne (f) — channel

chaîne (f) de proximité
local TV channel

chaîne (f) éducative
educational channel

chaîne (f) numérique — digital channel

chaîne (f) payante
subscription channel

couverture (f) intensive
blanket coverage

crypté/e — scrambled

décodeur (m) — decoder

diffuser — to broadcast

divertissant/e — entertaining

documentaire (m) — documentary

documentaire (m) animalier
wildlife documentary

documentaire (m) touristique
travel programme

doublé/e — dubbed

droits (mpl) d'antenne
television rights

émetteur (m) — transmitter

émission (f) — broadcast

émission (f) scolaire
schools programme

émission (f) sportive
sports programme

en différé — recorded, replay

en direct — live

en noir et blanc — black and white

équipe (f) de tournage — camera crew

flash (m) d'information — newsflash

flash (m) publicitaire
television advert

générique (m) — credits

grille (f) des programmes — schedule

heure (f) d'émission — broadcast time

heures (fpl) de grande écoute
peak viewing

image (f) défectueuse — poor picture

interruption (f) — interruption

lecteur (m) de DVD — DVD player

local/e — local

long métrage (m) — feature film

magnétoscope (m) — video recorder

moyen (m) d'évasion — form of escape

nullité (f) — flop

numérique — digital

passer à l'antenne	to go on the air
perturbation (f)	disturbance
présentateur/présentatrice (m/f)	announcer
primé/e	award-winning
programmation (f)	programming
programme (m) bas de gamme	downmarket programme
programme (m) haut de gamme	upmarket programme
public-cible (m)	target audience
qualité (f) de l'image	picture quality
questions (fpl) d'actualité	current affairs
réalisation (f)	production
réception (f)	reception
recevoir#	to receive
redevance (f)	licence
rediffusion (f)	repeat
régional/e	local
reprise (f)	repeat
réseau (m)	network
série (f) culte	cult series
société (f) de télévision	television company
speaker/speakerine (m/f)	announcer
super-production (f)	blockbuster
taux (m) d'écoute	viewing figures

télé-poubelle (f)	trash-television, rubbish
téléachat (m)	TV shopping
télécommande (f)	remote control
téléspectateur/trice (m/f)	viewer
télétexte (m)	Teletext
téléthon (m)	fund-raising TV programme for charity
télévision (f) du matin	breakfast television
télévision (f) en couleurs	colour television
télévision (f) interactive	interactive television
télévision (f) numérique	digital television
télévision (f) par câble	cable television
télévision (f) par satellite	satellite television
transmettre#	to transmit
valeur (f) éducative	educational value
vidéocassette (f) à caractère pornographique	pornographic video nasty
vidéocassette (f) à caractère violent	video nasty
village (m) global	global village
zapper	to channel-hop
zapping (m)	channel-hopping

la banalisation de la violence	making violence a commonplace event
changer# de chaîne	to change channels
faire# de la publicité à la télévision	to advertise on television

la course à l'audience	*competition for viewers*
parler en utilisant des phrases toutes faites	*to talk in sound-bites*
une fenêtre ouverte sur le monde	*an open window on the world*
regarder l'histoire en train de se faire	*to watch history in the making*
sous-titré/e pour les mal-entendants	*subtitled for the hard of hearing*
rester cloué/e devant la télévision	*to sit glued in front of the television*
diffusé/e en direct dans le salon	*beamed straight into the living room*
un/e envoyé/e permanent/e à l'étranger	*foreign correspondent*
notre envoyé/e spécial/e	*our special correspondent*
être câblé	*to have cable television*
l'emprise de la télé sur	*the hold that television has over*
sous forme numérique	*in digital format*

LA RADIO

audimat (*m*)	*ratings*	longueur (*f*) d'ondes		*wavelength*
auditeur/auditrice (*m/f*)	*listener*	personnalité (*f*) de la radio		*broadcaster*
audition (*f*)	*reception*	pièce (*f*) radiophonique		*radio play*
bande (*f*) de fréquences	*waveband*	présentateur/présentatrice (*m/f*)		*presenter*
brancher sur	*to tune into*	radio (*f*) libre		*commercial radio station*
capter	*to pick up*	radiodiffusion (*f*)		*broadcasting*
disc-jockey (*m*)	*disc-jockey*	reportage (*m*)		*report*
fond (*m*) sonore	*background noise*	son (*m*)		*sound*
fréquence (*f*)	*frequency*	station (*f*) de radio		*radio station*
interviewer (*m*)	*interviewer*	stéréo (*f*)		*stereo*
intervieweuse (*f*)	*interviewer*	sur grandes ondes		*on long wave*
jingle (*m*)	*signature tune*			

vous êtes à l'écoute de France-Inter	*you are listening to France-Inter*
c'est Jean Lebrun au micro	*the presenter is Jean Lebrun*
écouter une émission en modulation de fréquence	*to listen to a VHF/FM broadcast*

LA PRESSE

abonnement (*m*)	subscription
abonné/e (*m/f*)	subscriber
agence (*f*) de presse	press agency
annonce (*f*)	announcement
article (*m*)	article
article (*m*) de tête	leader, editorial
autorégulation (*f*)	self-regulation
chroniqueur/euse (*m/f*)	columnist
collaborateur/trice (*m/f*)	contributor
communiqué (*m*) de presse	press release
conférence (*f*) de presse	press conference
droit (*m*) d'auteur	copyright
coquille (*f*)	misprint
courrier (*m*) du cœur	agony column
de caractère (*m*) diffamatoire	libellous
diffamation (*f*)	libel
diffusion (*f*)	circulation
divertir	to amuse
éditeur/trice (*m/f*)	publisher
enquête (*f*)	investigation
envoyé/e (*m/f*) spécial/e	special correspondent
équipe (*f*) de rédaction	editorial team
exemplaire (*m*)	copy
faits divers (*mpl*)	news in brief
grand public (*m*)	the general public
gros titre (*m*)	headline
hebdomadaire (*m*)	weekly (also adj)
illustré (*m*)	magazine
imprimer	to print
journal (*m*) du dimanche	Sunday newspaper
journal (*m*) plein format	broadsheet
journal (*m*) sérieux	quality newspaper
journalisme (*m*) d'enquête	investigative journalism
lectorat (*m*)	readership
liberté (*f*) de la presse	freedom of the press
mensuel/le	monthly
mise (*f*) en page	layout
nombre (*m*) de lecteurs	readership
objectif/ve	objective
petites annonces (*fpl*)	small ads
pigiste (*m/f*)	freelance journalist
prix (*m*) de revient	cost price
publier	to publish
quotidien (*m*) populaire	tabloid daily
rédacteur/trice (*m/f*)	editor
reportage (*m*)	report
reportage (*m*) exclusif	an exclusive
revue (*f*) de luxe	glossy magazine
revue (*f*) professionnelle	trade magazine
rubrique (*f*)	section
rubrique (*f*) affaires	business section
rubrique (*f*) des spectacles	entertainments column
rubrique (*f*) sportive	sports pages
supplément (*m*)	supplement
supplément (*m*) en couleurs	colour supplement
téléscripteur (*m*)	teleprinter
tirage (*m*)	circulation
zone (*f*) de diffusion	circulation area

s'abonner à	to take out a subscription to
tenir# le lecteur au courant	to keep the reader informed
garantir la libre parole	to guarantee free speech
faire# la une	to make the front page/headlines
la presse à sensation	the gutter press
essayer# de museler la presse	to try to muzzle the press
un journal à grand tirage	mass circulation newspaper
s'ingérer# dans la vie privée de quelqu'un	to intrude on somebody's privacy
un journaliste en herbe	a budding journalist

LA PUBLICITÉ

acheteur/euse (m/f)	buyer
affiche (f)	poster
agence (f) de publicité	advertising agency
annonce (f)	advertisement
campagne (f) promotionnelle	advertising campaign
campagne (f) publicitaire	advertising campaign
cibler	to target
client/e (m/f)	customer
clientèle (f)	the customers
concurrence (f)	competition
déformer la réalité	to distort the truth
échantillon (m) gratuit	free sample
efficace	effective
embarras (m) du choix	too much choice
étude (f) de marché	market survey
évoquer	to evoke, to conjure up
exagération (f)	exaggeration
exploité/e	exploited
faire# appel à	to appeal to
image (f) de marque	brand image
informatif/ve	informative
insidieux/euse	insidious, underhand
invraisemblable	unlikely, implausible
journal (m) gratuit	free paper
lettre (f) personnalisée	mail-shot
marque (f)	make, brand
mensongère	deceitful
mentir#	to lie
normes (fpl) publicitaires	advertising standards
panneau (m) d'affichage	billboard
partial/e	prejudiced
publicitaires (m/fpl)	advertising executives
publicité (f) cinématographique	cinema advertising
publicité (f) radiodiffusée	radio advertising
publicité (f) télévisuelle	TV advertising
réclame (f)	advertisement
ritournelle (f) publicitaire	jingle
slogan (m)	slogan
snobisme (m)	snobbery
spot (m) publicitaire	commercial break
usage (m) de l'érotisme	use of sex
ventes (fpl) accrues	increased sales

tenir# compte des réalités	*to take into account the facts*
exploiter le sexe	*to exploit sex*
un produit de consommation courante	*an everyday item*
se laisser manipuler par	*to let oneself be manipulated by*
pour ne pas être# en reste avec les voisins	*to keep up with the Jones's*
au-delà des moyens de	*beyond the (financial) means of*
une incitation à consommer	*an encouragement to consumption*
une société de consommation	*a consumer society*
inciter à dépenser de l'argent	*to encourage you to spend your money*
agir sur le subconscient	*to act on the subconscious*
faire# appel à nos instincts primitifs	*to appeal to our base instincts*
le lavage de cerveau	*brainwashing*
le revenu publicitaire	*advertising revenue*
faire# connaître un produit	*to get a product known*
influencer le comportement d'achat	*to influence buying behaviour*
le parrainage publicitaire	*advertising sponsorship*

DIVERS

bienfaits (*mpl*)	*the benefits*
censure (*f*)	*censorship*
compréhension (*f*)	*understanding*
conscience (*f*) de	*awareness of*
crénau (*m*)	*niche*
diffuser	*to broadcast, disseminate*
l'écrit (*m*)	*the written word*
ère (*f*) du multimédia	*the multimedia age*
s'exprimer	*to express oneself*
influencer#	*to influence*
instruire#	*to educate*

liberté (*f*) d'information	*freedom of information*
liberté (*f*) de parole	*freedom of speech*
les mass médias (*mpl*)	*the mass media*
médiatiquement	*through/by the media*
médiatisation (*f*)	*promotion through the media*
nocif/ve	*harmful*
nuisible	*harmful*
pornographique	*pornographic*
propagande (*f*)	*propaganda*

un code de bonne conduite	*a code of good conduct*
la mise en orbite de	*the launch of (a product, magazine, etc.)*
le scandale est un thème vendeur	*scandal boosts sales*
obtenir# une bonne couverture médiatique	*to get good media coverage*
un événement médiatique	*a media event*
un homme informé en vaut deux	*forewarned is forearmed (Proverb)*
selon des sources bien informées	*according to well-informed sources*
l'opium du peuple	*the opium of the people*
les publications pour les jeunes	*teenage publications*

SITES INTERNET UTILES

www.club-internet.fr/medias

www.tf1.fr (site de TF1 en France)

www.francealacarte.org.uk (le site du réseau culturel français au Royaume-Uni)

http://globegate.utm.edu/french/topics/tv.and.radio.html (une liste de sites sur la télé et la radio francophones)

http://globegate.utm.edu/french/topics/newspapers.html (une liste de sites des journaux francophones)

www.swarthmore.edu/Humanities/clicnet/presse.ecrite.html (la presse francophone)

www.ambafrance.org/KIOSQUE/fran.html (des liens à la presse)

www.ucad.fr/pub/ (le site du musée de la publicité)

www.comfm.fr (des liens aux médias)

www.liberation.fr (site du journal)

www.phosphore.com (le site du magazine pour les 15-25 ans)

www.france2.fr/evenements (les actualités)

www.grolier.fr/studio (des infos sur les médias)

http://perso.wanadoo.fr/olivier-c/AnnuaireWeb.html (des adresses sur les médias)

LES PROBLÈMES SOCIAUX

LE CHÔMAGE

allocation (f) de chômage
unemployment benefit

augmentation (f)   *increase*

blocage (m) des salaires   *pay freeze*

bureau (m) d'embauche
unemployment office

chiffre (m)   *figure*

chômage (m) des jeunes
youth unemployment

chômeur/euse (m/f)
unemployed person

confiance (f) en soi   *self-confidence*

débaucher   *to lay off staff*

dégradation (f)   *worsening*

demandeur/euse (m/f) d'emploi
job-seeker

désœuvrement (m)
lack of anything to do

embauche (f)   *vacancy*

ennui (m)   *boredom*

facteur (m)   *factor*

grève (f)   *strike*

grève (f) du zèle   *work-to-rule*

grève (f) patronale   *lockout*

grève (f) totale   *all-out strike*

gréviste (m/f)   *striker*

impuissance (f)   *powerlessness*

inactifs (mpl)
the numbers unemployed

jaune (m)   *scab*

licenciement (m)   *dismissal*

marché (m) de l'emploi
the jobs market

marché (m) du travail   *labour market*

partage (m) de poste   *job-sharing*

population (f) active
active population

préavis (m) de grève   *strike notice*

reconversion (f)   *retraining*

respect (m) de soi   *self-esteem*

Rmiste (m)
someone on income support

robotisation (f)   *automation*

sans-emploi (mpl)   *the jobless*

statistiques (fpl)   *statistics*

suppressions (fpl) d'emploi   *jobs lost*

supprimer   *to do away with*

taux (m) de chômage
unemployment level

travail (m) à temps partiel
part-time work

variation (f) saisonnière
seasonal variation

mettre# quelqu'un en/au chômage   *to make someone redundant*

plan (m) de création d'emplois   *job creation scheme*

décommander une grève   *to call off a strike*

avoir# de l'impact sur	*to have an impact on*
les chômeurs de longue durée	*the long-term unemployed*
une diminution de la semaine de travail	*a reduction in the working week*
réduire# l'âge de la retraite	*to bring down the retirement age*
des entreprises en pleine mutation	*companies undergoing radical change*
s'inscrire# au chômage	*to sign on the dole*
le nombre d'actifs	*the number of those in work*
recevoir# l'aide sociale	*to be on social security*
le revenu minimum d'insertion (RMI)	*income support*
la prime de licensiement	*redundancy money*
le chômage endémique	*chronic unemployment*
renvoyer des salariés	*to dismiss employees*
travailler au noir	*to moonlight*
inadapté/e au travail	*unsuitable for work*
l'incapacité de travail	*industrial disability*
parrainer un chômeur	*to sponsor an unemployed person*
traverser une période difficile	*to go through a bad patch*
une classe sociale très défavorisée	*a social underclass*

LES SANS-ABRI

s'abriter	*to shelter*
affamé/e	*starving*
Armée (*f*) du Salut	*Salvation Army*
aumône (*f*)	*handout*
bénévolat (*m*)	*voluntary help*
bénévole (*mf*)	*voluntary helper*
caritatif/ve	*charitable*
cité (*m*) de transit	*(temporary) hostel*
clochard (*m*)	*tramp*
collecte (*f*) de fonds	*fund-raising*
déchéance (*f*)	*decline*
défavorisés (*mpl*)	*the disadvantaged*
démunis (*mpl*)	*the destitute*
dénuement (*m*)	*destitution*
désavantagés (*mpl*)	*the underprivileged*
désespoir (*m*)	*despair*
déshérités (*mpl*)	*the have-nots*
dignité (*f*)	*dignity*
exclusion (*f*) sociale	*social exclusion*
expulser	*to evict*
foyer (*m*)	*hostel*
gêne (*f*)	*financial difficulties*
gens (*mpl*) du voyage	*travellers (e.g. New Age)*
honte (*f*)	*shame*
inadapté/e (*m/f*)	*misfit*
indésirable	*undesirable*

malades (*mpl*) mentaux   *the mentally ill*

marginaliser   *to exclude from society*

marginaux (*mpl*)
  people living on the fringes of society

mendicité (*f*)   *begging*

misère (*f*)   *extreme poverty*

musicien/ne (*m/f*) des rues   *busker*

nécessiteux/euse   *needy*

organismes (*mpl*) caritatifs/
  œuvres (*fpl*) charitables   *charities*

parasite (*m*)   *scrounger*

paupérisation (*f*)   *impoverishment*

pauvreté (*f*)   *poverty*

personne (*f*) absente   *missing person*

quart monde (*m*)   *underclass*

quartiers (*mpl*) déshérités
  inner-city areas

réinsérer   *to rehabilitate*

réinsertion (*f*)   *reintegration*

sans-abri (*mpl*)   *the homeless*

scandale (*m*)   *scandal*

seuil (*m*) de pauvreté   *poverty line*

société (*f*) d'abondance
  the affluent society

soupe (*f*) populaire   *soup kitchen*

squatter   *to squat*

travail (*m*) social   *social work*

vulnérable   *vulnerable*

les naufragés de la conjoncture	*the casualties of the economic situation*
emménager# sur le bitume	*to live/sleep rough*
la ville se clochardise	*the town has more and more homeless people*
dormir# sous les ponts	*to live in cardboard boxes*
recevoir# l'aide sociale	*to be on social security*
hébergement (*m*) d'urgence	*emergency accommodation*
impropre à l'habitation	*not fit for human habitation*
Les SDF (sans domicile fixe)	*those of no fixed abode*
l'isolement (*m*) social	*social isolation*
faire# une fugue	*to run away from home*
à l'écart de la société	*on the margins of society*
les restos du coeur	*meal centres for the homeless*
l'allocation au logement	*housing benefit*
les exclus	*people cut off from mainstream society*
la fracture sociale	*the break-up of society*
réintégrer le monde du travail	*to return to the world of work*
se réintégrer dans la société	*to rejoin mainstream society*

LE CRIME

acte (*m*) délictueux	*criminal act*
affrontement (*m*)	*confrontation*
agresser	*to attack*
agresseur (*m*)	*attacker*
armes (*fpl*) à poing	*handguns/knives*
s'attaquer à	*to attack*
atteinte (*f*)	*attack*
bagarre (*f*)	*brawl*
se bagarrer avec	*to brawl*
balle (*f*)	*bullet*
braquage (*m*)	*hold-up*
braqueur (*m*)	*gangster*
brigade (*f*) criminelle	*crime squad*
butin (*m*)	*booty, haul*
cambriolage (*m*)	*burglary*
casse (*m*)	*break-in*
chantage (*m*)	*blackmail*
chasse (*f*) à l'homme	*manhunt*
châtiment (*m*)	*punishment*
chien (*m*) de défense	*guard dog*
commettre#	*to commit*
complice (*m/f*)	*accomplice*
confisquer	*to confiscate*
crapules (*fpl*)	*scum, riffraff*
crime (*m*) passionnel	*crime of passion*
CRS (*f*)	*riot police*
se défendre	*to defend oneself*
dégrader	*to damage*
délinquance (*f*)	*criminality*
délit (*m*)	*offence*
détenir#	*to hold prisoner*

dévaliser/cambrioler	*to burgle*
écœurant/e	*sickening, disgusting*
élucider	*to clear up, to solve*
émeute (*f*)	*riot*
en flagrant délit	*red-handed*
endommager#	*to damage*
enlèvement (*m*)	*kidnapping*
escroc (*m*)	*crook*
faire# irruption	*to burst in*
forces (*fpl*) de l'ordre	*police*
fraude (*f*) fiscale	*tax evasion*
fusillade (*f*)	*gunfire*
garde (*f*) à vue	*police custody*
gardiennage (*m*)	*security*
groupe (*m*) d'autodéfense	*vigilante group*
incendie (*m*) criminel	*arson*
indicateur (*m*)	*informer*
infraction (*f*)	*offence, crime*
injurier	*to insult*
intrus (*m*)	*intruder*
ligoter	*to tie up*
malfaiteur (*m*)	*criminal*
mobile (*m*)	*motive*
otage (*m*)	*hostage*
pègre (*f*)	*underworld*
poignarder	*to stab*
police (*f*) de proximité	*community police*
port (*m*) d'armes	*gun licence*
prendre# la fuite	*to run away*
proxénétisme (*m*)	*pimping*

puce (*f*) électronique	*electronic tag*	sévir	*to be rife*
punition (*f*) corporelle		tagueur (*m*)	*grafitti artist*
	corporal punishment	témoin (*m*)	*witness*
racket (*m*)	*racketeering*	truand (*m*)	*crook*
racketter		vandalisme (*m*)	*vandalism*
	to extract money with menaces	viol (*m*)	*rape*
rafle (*f*)	*police raid*	violation (*f*) de domicile	
ravisseur/euse (*m/f*)			*forcible entry*
	kidnapper, abductor	violer	*to rape*
recel (*m*)	*receiving stolen goods*	vol (*m*) à l'étalage	*shoplifting*
règlement (*m*) de comptes		vol (*m*) à la roulotte	*theft from cars*
	settling of scores	vol (*m*) à la tire	*pickpocketing*
réinsérer	*to rehabilitate*	vol (*m*) à main armée	*armed robbery*
relâcher	*to set free*	vols (*mpl*) de voiture	*car theft*
repris (*m*) de justice	*ex-convict*	voyou (*m*)	*hooligan*
saccager#	*to ransack*		

faire# une virée	*to go joyriding*
prendre# en otage	*to take hostage*
la vague de criminalité	*the crime wave*
être# à l'abri de la violence	*to be safe from violence*
exercer# un effet de dissuasion	*to act as a deterrent*
se porter au secours de quelqu'un	*to go to someone's aid*
face à la recrudescence de la violence	*faced with the increased tide of violence*
déborder en violence	*to spill over into violence*
est-il souhaitable que la police soit armée?	*is it desirable to arm the police?*
agir sous l'emprise de l'alcool	*to act under the influence of alcohol*
la lutte contre le crime	*crime prevention*
punir plus durement	*to punish more severely*
une flambée de violence	*an outburst of violence*
devenir le caïd du quartier	*to become top dog in the area*
les déconnectés de la société	*people alienated from society*
les malaises sociaux	*social unrest*

la cohésion sociale	*social cohesion*
la réinsertion sociale des anciens détenus	*the rehabilitation of ex-prisoners*
la délinquance juvénile	*juvenile delinquency*
le taux de criminalité	*the crime rate*
être# en infraction	*to be in breach of the law*
un attentat à la pudeur	*indecent assault*
la surpopulation des prisons	*prison overcrowding*

LA JUSTICE

accusé/e (*m/f*)	*accused*
acquitter qn	*to find somebody innocent*
amende (*f*)	*fine*
arrêté (*m*) municipal	*bye-law*
assermenté/e	*on oath*
atténuant/e	*mitigating*
attester	*to give evidence*
avocat/e (*m/f*)	*lawyer*
casier (*m*) judiciaire	*criminal record*
Code (*m*) Pénal	*penal code*
condamner	*to sentence*
contravention (*f*)	*motoring fine*
coupable	*guilty*
cour (*f*) d'appel	*court of appeal*
cour (*f*) de cassation	*final court of appeal*
défenseur (*m*)	*defence counsel*
déposition (*f*)	*statement*
détenu (*m*)	*prison inmate*
écrouer	*to imprison*
emprisonnement (*m*)	*imprisonment*
être# sous les verrous	*to be behind bars*
incarcération (*f*)	*imprisonment*
inculper de	*to accuse of*
juge (*m*) d'instruction	*examining magistrate*
juridiquement	*legally*
libération (*f*) conditionnelle	*release on parole*
ordre (*m*) public	*law and order*
parquet (*m*)	*public prosecutor's office*
pénitentiaire	*prison (adj)*
plaider coupable	*to plead guilty*
plaidoirie (*f*)	*defence speech*
population (*f*) carcérale	*the prison population*
procès (*m*)	*trial*
processus (*m*) judiciaire	*legal process*
procureur (*m*)	*state prosecutor*
poursuivre# quelqu'un	*to prosecute somebody*
récidiver	*to reoffend*

récidiviste (m)   *habitual offender*
réclusion à perpétuité
   life imprisonment
salle (f) d'audience   *courtroom*
sous caution   *on bail*
système (m) pénal   *penal system*
témoin (m)   *witness*
tribunal (m)   *court*

tribunal (m) correctionnel
   magistrates' court
tribunal (m) pour enfants
   juvenile court
venger#   *to avenge*
violation (f) de la loi
   breaking the law

condamné/e à l'emprisonnement à perpétuité — *given a life sentence*
en détention provisoire — *remanded in custody*
comparaître# devant le tribunal — *to appear in court*
ouvrir# une information — *to start a preliminary investigation*
sanctionner une contravention — *to punish a crime*
un an de prison avec sursis — *a one-year suspended sentence*
le crime ne paie pas — *crime doesn't pay*
intenter un procès à — *to start proceedings against*
cela touche à la liberté de chacun — *this affects the freedom of everyone*
la cour européenne des droits de l'homme — *the European court of human rights*
mettre# en garde à vue — *to take into custody*
une erreur judiciaire — *a miscarriage of justice*
gagner/perdre son procès — *to win/lose one's case*
engager des poursuites judiciaires contre — *to take legal proceedings against*
abandonner les poursuites — *to drop the charges*
toute personne est présumée innocente jusqu'à ce qu'elle soit jugée coupable — *everyone is presumed innocent until proven guilty*

LE TERRORISME

assassin (m)   *killer*
assassiner   *to murder*
atrocité (f)   *outrage*
attentat (m)   *attack*

attentat (m) à la bombe   *bomb attack*
balle (f)   *bullet*
bombe (f) télécommandée
   remote-controlled bomb
cellule (f)   *(terrorist) cell*
cible (f)   *target*

71

dépister	to track down
désamorcer#	to defuse
détourner	to hijack
faire# sauter	to blow up
impitoyable	ruthless
indicateur (*m*) de police	informer, supergrass
innocent/e	innocent
mesures (*fpl*) de sécurité	security measures
meurtrier/ière	deadly, lethal
militant/e (*m/f*)	activist
organisation (f) clandestine	secret organisation

otage (*m*)	hostage
perpétrer#	to carry out
piégé/e	booby-trapped
plastiquer	to carry out a bomb attack on
plastiqueur (*m*)	bomber
poser une bombe	to plant a bomb
reculer	to back down
revendiquer	to claim
sympathisant/e (*m/f*)	sympathiser
terroriste (*m/f*)	terrorist
tirer sur	to open fire on
tireur (*m*) isolé	sniper
voiture (*f*) piégée	car-bomb

faire# la grève de la faim	to go on hunger strike
créer des martyrs	to create martyrs
un meurtre commis de sang-froid	a cold-blooded murder
un acte délibéré de terrorisme	a calculated act of terrorism
prendre# des mesures énergiques contre	to crack down on
interdire# l'accès à	to cordon off
un attentat commis au hasard	a random attack
désamorcer une bombe	to defuse a bomb
faire# voler en éclats	to blow to smithereens
revendiquer la responsabilité de l'attentat	to claim responsibility for the attack
perpétrer# un attentat	to carry out an attack
renforcer la sécurité	to step up security
provoquer d'importants dégâts	to cause extensive damage
une prison de haute sécurité	top security prison

LA PEINE DE MORT

abolir	to abolish
appliquer	to apply
assassinat (*m*)	murder
barbare	barbaric

chaise (*f*) électrique	electric chair
châtiment (*m*) suprême	supreme penalty
chrétien/ne	Christian
condamnation (*f*) à mort	death sentence

à controverse	*controversial*
crime (*m*) odieux	*horrible crime*
crime (*m*) pendable	*hanging offence*
désaxé/e (*m/f*)	*unbalanced person*
dignité (*f*)	*dignity*
éliminer	*to eliminate*
exécution (*f*)	*execution*
faire# revivre	*to bring back to life*
gracier	*to pardon*
guillotiner	*to send to the guillotine*
homicide (*m*) involontaire	
	manslaughter

irréversible	*irreversible*
maladie (*f*) mentale	*mental illness*
meurtrier/ière (*m/f*)	
	murderer/murderess
moratoire (*m*)	*moratorium*
peine (*f*) capitale	*capital punishment*
pendaison (*f*)	*hanging*
prison (*f*) à vie	*life imprisonment*
punition (*f*)	*punishment*
rétablir	*to restore*
rétablissement (*m*)	
	restoration, restoring

avoir# un effet dissuasif sur	*to act as a deterrent for*
condamner quelqu'un à mort	*to condemn someone to death*
accorder une commutation de la peine capitale	*to grant a reprieve*
les infractions passibles de la peine de mort	*crimes which carry the death penalty*
avoir# une limite sur l'âge	*to have an age limit*
le droit de la société de se défendre	*society's right to defend itself*
une erreur judiciaire	*a miscarriage of justice*
le quartier des condamnés à mort	*'death row'*
des circonstances atténuantes	*mitigating circumstances*
supprimer la peine de mort	*to do away with the death penalty*

SITES INTERNET UTILES

www.terra.fr (site des Restos du Coeur)

www.conseil-etat.fr (site sur la justice en France)

www.justice.gouv.fr (site du ministère de la justice en France)

www.msp.gouv.qc.ca/index (site sur la sécurité publique au Canada)

http://globegate.utm.edu/franch/globegate_mirror/law.html

www.pratique.fr (site sur la justice)

73

LA SANTÉ

LA DROGUE

abus (*m*) de drogue	*drug abuse*
accoutumance (*f*) à la drogue	*drug habit*
accro	*hooked*
acide (*m*)	*acid*
s'adonner à	*to become addicted to*
battage (*m*)	*hype*
brigade (*f*) des stupéfiants	*Drug Squad*
camé/e (*m/f*)	*junkie*
campagne (*f*) d'information	*information campaign*
cannabis (*m*)	*cannabis*
cocaïne (*f*)	*cocaine*
colle (*f*)	*glue*
comateux/euse	*comatose*
consommateur/trice (*m*) de drogue	*drug-taker*
crack (*m*)	*crack*
dangerosité (*f*)	*level of danger*
dealer (*m*)	*drug pusher*
décrocher	*to come off drugs*
dépénaliser	*to decriminalise*
dépendance (*f*) à	*dependency on*
désintoxiquer	*to treat for drug addiction*
disponibilité (*f*)	*availability*
drogue (*f*) de synthèse	*designer drug*
drogue (*f*) douce/dure	*soft/hard drug*
drogue-partie (*f*)	*drugs party*
drogué/e (*m/f*)	*drug addict*
se droguer	*to take drugs*
enrayer#	*to curb, put a stop to*
euphorie (*f*)	*euphoria*
expérimentation (*f*)	*experimentation*
gélule (*f*)	*capsule*
hachisch (*m*)	*hashish*
hallucination (*f*)	*halllucination*
héroïne (*f*)	*heroin*
héroïnemanie (*f*)	*heroin addiction*
illicite	*illicit*
s'injecter	*to inject oneself*
joint (*m*)	*joint*
légaliser	*to legalise*
lutte (*f*) anti-drogue	*battle against drugs*
marie-jeanne (*f*)	*pot*
marijuana (*m*)	*marijuana*
méfaits (*mpl*)	*ill-effects*
milieu (*m*) de la drogue	*drug scene*
nocif/ive	*harmful*
overdose (*f*)	*overdose*
se piquer	*to inject oneself*
planer	*to be high on drugs*
poussée (*f*) de stupéfiants	*drug-pushing*
prise (*f*)	*seizure*

répandu/e	*widespread*	stupéfiant (*m*)	*drug*
répression (*f*) contre	*crackdown on*	toxico (toxicomane) (*m/f*)	*drug addict*
revendeur (*m*) de drogue	*drug peddler*	toxicomanie (*f*)	*drug addiction*
saisie (*f*) de drogue	*drugs haul*	trafic (*m*) de la drogue	
sequelles (*fpl*)	*after-effects*		*drug-trafficking*
seringue (*f*)	*syringe*	trafiquant (*m*)	*drug smuggler*
se shooter à quelque chose		traitement (*m*)	*treatment*
	to mainline something	usage (*m*) de la drogue	*drug-taking*
sniffeur (*m*)	*glue-sniffer*	usager (*m*) de drogue	*drug user*

proposer de la drogue	*to offer drugs*
être# asservi/e à la drogue	*to be a slave to drugs*
une pente fatale	*a slippery slope*
se prémunir contre	*to guard against*
faire# un trip qui tourne mal	*to have a bad trip*
le désir de goûter au fruit défendu	*the wish to taste forbidden fruit*
s'échapper de la vie contemporaine	*to escape from modern life*
sombrer dans le désespoir	*to sink into despair*
lever# l'interdiction sur	*to lift the ban on*
la poursuite de nouvelles sensations	*the pursuit of new sensations*
reconnaître# les symptômes	*to spot the symptoms*
sniffer de la colle	*to glue sniff*
subir un violent contre-coup physique	*to suffer violent physical after-effects*
l'usage de solvants hallucinogènes	*solvent abuse*
accusé de laxisme à l'égard des drogues	*accused of being too soft on drugs*
s'enfermer dans un cercle vicieux	*to get into a vicious circle*
être# en état de manque	*to experience withdrawal symptoms*
les pays producteurs	*countries where drugs are grown*
une seringue usagée	*a used syringe*
fumer de l'herbe	*to smoke pot*
un changement de personnalité	*a personality change*
faire# une cure de désintoxication	*to be treated for drug addiction*
empêcher les rechutes chez les toxicomanes	*to prevent addicts from backsliding*

L'ALCOOL

alcoolique (*m/f*)	*alcoholic*
alcoolisme (*m*)	*alcoholism*
Alcootest (*m*)	*Breathalyser*
arroser	*to celebrate with alcohol*
avertissement (*m*)	*warning*
beuverie (*f*)	*drinking bout, binge*
boire# à l'excès	*to drink excessively*
boire# beaucoup	*to be a heavy drinker*
boisson (*f*) alcoolisée	*alcoholic drink*
boisson (*f*) légèrement alcoolisée	*low alcohol drink*
boisson (*f*) non alcoolisée	*soft drink*
buveur/euse (*m/f*)	*drinker*
canette (*f*) de bière	*bottle of beer*
cirrhose (*f*) du foie	*cirrhosis of the liver*
coordination (*f*)	*co-ordination*
corser	*to spike a drink*
dégriser	*to sober up*

délier la langue	*to loosen your tongue*
ébriété (*f*)	*intoxication*
s'enivrer	*to get drunk*
éthylisme (*m*)	*alcoholism*
s'évanouir	*to blackout*
excessif/ve	*excessive*
inadaptation (*f*)	*maladjustment*
inhibition (*f*)	*inhibition*
ivresse (*f*)	*drunkenness*
ivrogne (*m/f*)	*drunkard*
régime (*m*) sec	*alcohol-free diet*
sobre	*sober*
taux (*m*) légal	*legal limit*
teneur (*f*) en alcool	*alcoholic strength*
tournée (*f*)	*round of drinks*
trembler	*to have the shakes*
trinquer à la santé de quelqu'un	*to toast someone*
unité (*f*) d'alcool	*unit of alcohol*
verre (*m*)	*drink*

avec modération	*in moderation*
s'abstenir# de boire	*to refrain from drink*
l'alcool au volant	*drink driving*
le taux d'alcoolémie	*alcohol level in the bloodstream*
la consommation d'alcool par les mineurs	*under-age drinking*
faire# la tournée des bars	*to go on a pub crawl*
perdre# tout contrôle de soi	*to lose all self-control*
être# en état d'ébriété	*to be under the influence of alcohol*
une personne qui ne boit jamais d'alcool	*teetotaler*
faire# régresser l'alcoolisme	*to reduce alcoholism*
enrayer# l'alcoolisme	*to eliminate alcoholism*

avoir# la gueule de bois	*to have a hangover*
les lois réglementant la vente d'alcool	*the licensing laws*
une cure de désintoxication	*a drying-out treatment*
en état d'ivresse publique	*drunk and disorderly*
facilement disponible	*readily available*
l'abus d'alcool chez les jeunes	*excessive drinking amongst the young*
un coma éthylique	*an alcoholic coma*
sous l'influence de l'alcool	*under the influence of alcohol*
l'empoisonnement alcoolique	*alcohol poisoning*
se faire# désintoxiquer	*to dry out*
les heures d'ouverture légales	*opening hours*

L'ALIMENTATION

additif (*m*)	*additive*
aliments (*mpl*) diététiques	*health-foods*
aliments (*mpl*) organiques	*wholefoods*
allégé/e	*low-fat*
anorexie (*f*)	*anorexia*
biologique	*natural, organic*
boulimie (*f*)	*bulimia*
calorie (*f*)	*calory*
cholestérol (*m*)	*cholesterol*
colorant (*m*) artificiel	*artificial colouring*
conservateur (*m*)	*preservative*
conserves (*fpl*)	*tinned foods*
cuisine (*f*) minceur	*lean cuisine*
éviter	*to avoid*
excès (*m*)	*excess*
grossir	*to put on weight*
intoxication (*f*) alimentaire	*food poisoning*
laitages (*mpl*)	*milk products*
ligne (*f*)	*figure*
maigrir	*to lose weight*
matière (*f*) grasse	*fat content*
modération (*f*)	*moderation*
obèse	*obese*
obsédé/e	*obsessed*
se peser#	*to weigh oneself*
peser# trop	*to be overweight*
se régaler	*to have a lovely meal*
restauration (*f*) rapide	*fast food*
sous-vide	*vacuum-packed*
sucreries (*fpl*)	*sugary foods*
se suralimenter	*to overeat*
transgénique	*genetically modified*
vitamine (*f*)	*vitamin*

l'hygiène alimentaire	*food hygiene*
manger# plus sainement	*to eat more healthily*
grignoter entre les repas	*to nibble between meals*
se mettre# au régime	*to go on a diet*
suivre# un régime sain	*to eat a healthy diet*
la valeur nutritive	*nutritional value*
riche/pauvre en calories	*with a high/low calorie content*
riche/pauvre en fibres	*high/low in fibre*
les OGM (organismes génétiquement modifiés)	*genetically modified crops*
des produits garantis sans OGM	*no genetically modified ingredients*
un magasin diététique	*a health-food shop*
avoir# une alimentation équilibrée	*to eat a balanced diet*
sauter un repas	*to skip a meal*
des troubles de l'alimentation	*eating disorders*
diminuer la consommation de	*to cut down on*
se laisser mourir de faim	*to starve oneself to death*
surveiller son poids	*to be a weightwatcher*
la maladie de la vache folle	*mad cow disease*

LE TABAC

altérer la santé	*to impair your health*
bronchite (*f*) chronique	*chronic bronchitis*
calmer les nerfs	*to calm one's nerves*
cancer (*m*) des poumones	*lung cancer*
cancérigène	*carcinogenic*
dépendant/e de	*dependent upon*
difficulté (*f*) respiratoire	*breathing difficulties*
enfumer	*to fill with smoke*
espérance (*f*) de vie	*life expectancy*

éteindre#	*to extinguish*
évitable	*avoidable*
fumée (*f*) ambiante	*passive smoking*
fumeur/euse (*m/f*) invétéré/e	*chain-smoker*
gêner	*to disturb, bother*
habitude (*f*)	*habit*
haleine (*f*)	*breath*
haleter	*to gasp for breath*
inhaler	*to inhale*
interdiction (*f*)	*ban*
intoxiquer	*to poison*

lieu (*m*) public	*public place*
méfaits (*mpl*)	*ill effects*
néfaste	*harmful*
non-fumeur (*m*)	*non-smoker*
se passer de	*to do without*
patch (*m*)	*anti-smoking patch*
provoquer	*to cause*
rechuter	*to relapse*

régulièrement	*regularly*
renoncer à	*to give up*
supprimer	*to ban*
tabagisme (*m*)	
addiction to smoking, nicotine addiction	
taux (*m*) de nicotine	*nicotine level*
toux (*f*) de fumeur	*smoker's cough*

affirmer leur émancipation	*to prove their liberation*
la campagne anti-tabac	*the anti-smoking campaign*
essayer# d'arrêter	*to try to give up*
le risque de mort subite	*the risk of sudden death*
chez les gros fumeurs	*for heavy smokers*
une méthode de sevrage tabagique	*a way of weaning people off smoking*
prévenir# les jeunes des dangers	*to warn young people of the dangers*
le respect pour son propre organisme	*respect for one's own body*
dissuader les jeunes de fumer	*to put young people off smoking*
le tabac est nuisible à la santé	*smoking is harmful to your health*
les affres du manque	*withdrawal symptoms*
agir sans aucun égard envers autrui	*to act without any consideration for other people*
l'abandon du tabac	*giving up smoking*
abandonner la cigarette	*to stop smoking*
les conséquences de la fumée ambiante	*the results of passive smoking*

LE SIDA

aiguille (*f*) souillée	*dirty needle*
anticorps (*m*)	*antibody*
contracter	*to catch*
dépistage (*m*)	*screening*
donneur/euse (*m/f*) de sang	*blood donor*

épargner	*to spare*
épidémie (*f*)	*epidemic*
éthique	*ethical*
évitable	*avoidable*
éviter	*to avoid*
globule (*m*) blanc	*white blood cell*
guérissable	*curable*

hémophile (*m/f*)	*haemophiliac*
homosexuel	*homosexual*
hospice (*m*)	*hospice*
incurable	*incurable*
infecté/e	*infected*
infectieux/euse	*infectious*
irresponsable	*irresponsible*
partager#	*to share*
partenaires (*m/f*) multiples	
	multiple partners
population (*f*) à haut risque	
	high-risk group
porteur/euse (*m/f*)	*carrier*
pratiques (*mpl*) à risques	
	risky practices
préservatif (*m*)	*condom*
préventif/ve	*preventive*
promiscuité (*f*)	*promiscuity*
se propager	*to spread*
se protéger#	*to protect oneself*
rapports (*mpl*) sexuels protégés	
	safe sex
relations (*fpl*) sexuelles	*intercourse*

remède (*m*)	*cure*
ruban (*m*) rouge	*red ribbon*
sang (*m*) contaminé	
	contaminated blood
seringue (*f*)	*syringe*
séronégatif/ve	*HIV negative*
séropositif/ve	*HIV positive*
sexe (*m*) sans protection	
	unprotected sex
sidatique (*m/f*)	*AIDS victim*
sidéen/nne (*m/f*)	*AIDS sufferer*
survie (*f*)	*survival*
système (*m*) immunitaire	
	immune system
taux (*m*) de mortalité	*mortality rate*
transfusion (*f*) sanguine	
	blood transfusion
transmettre#	*to pass on*
transmission (*f*)	*transmission*
vaccin (*m*)	*vaccine*
victime (*f*)	*victim*
virus (*m*) HIV	*HIV virus*

les personnes atteintes par le SIDA	*people suffering from AIDS*
la propagation du SIDA	*the spread of AIDS*
lancer# un programme de sensibilisation	*to launch an awareness programme*
s'activer à la recherche d'un vaccin	*to be busy trying to find a vaccine*
changer# souvent de partenaire	*to change partners frequently*
modifier les habitudes sexuelles	*to change sexual habits*
déconseiller à quelqu'un de faire quelque chose	*to advise against*
un moyen de lutter contre le virus	*a means of combatting the virus*
la maladie peut se transmettre par	*the disease can be transmitted by*

NOUVELLES MÉDECINES ET ÉTHIQUE

avortement (*m*)	*abortion*
bébé-éprouvette (*m*)	*test-tube baby*
chercheur/euse (*m/f*)	*researcher*
clonage (*m*) humain	*human cloning*
cryogénie (*f*)	*cryogenics*
difforme	*deformed*
donneur (*m*)	*donor*
embryon (*m*)	*embryo*
épave (*f*)	*human vegetable*
éthique (*f*)	*(code of) ethics*
euthanasie (*f*)	*euthanasia*
fœtus (*m*)	*foetus*
gène (*m*)	*gene*
génétique (*f*)	*genetics*
greffe (*f*)	*transplant*
greffer	*to transplant*
immoral/e	*immoral*
lente agonie (*f*)	*lingering death*
mère (*f*) porteuse	*surrogate mother*
œuf (*m*) fécondé	*fertilised egg*
rein (*m*) artificiel	*artificial kidney*
respirateur (*m*) artificiel	*life-support machine*
stimulateur (*m*) cardiaque	*pacemaker*
sujet (*m*) délicat	*emotive issue*
surmédicalisation (*f*)	*over-reliance on medecines*

les manipulations génétiques	*genetic engineering*
poser des problèmes éthiques	*to cause ethical problems*
la procréation artificielle	*artificial insemination*
la fécondation in vitro (FIV)	*in vitro fertilisation (IVF)*
une transplantation cardiaque	*a heart transplant*
l'avortement est autorisé par la loi	*abortion is legally allowed*
supprimer un être humain	*to kill a human being*
une interruption volontaire de grossesse (IVG)	*an abortion*
une interruption thérapeutique de grossesse	*abortion on medical grounds*
la campagne contre l'avortement	*the anti-abortion campaign*
un avortement clandestin	*a back-street abortion*
être# en réanimation	*to be in intensive care*
une vie qui est à son terme	*a life which is at an end*
perdre l'envie de vivre	*to lose the will to live*
être# atteint/e d'un mal incurable	*to suffer from an incurable illness*
l'acharnement thérapeutique	*unnatural prolongation of life*
mourir# dans la dignité	*to die with dignity*
le testament de vie/testament biologique	*living will*

DIVERS

alité/e	*bedridden*
alléger#	*to relieve*
amiante (*f*)	*asbestos*
antidépresseur (*m*)	*antidepressant*
assurance (*f*) maladie	
	health insurance
atteint/e de	*suffering from*
automédication (*f*)	*self-medication*
aveugle	*blind*
avortée (*f*)	
	woman who has had an abortion
chien-guide (*m*)	*guide dog*
chimiothérapie (*f*)	*chemotherapy*
chirurgie (*f*) esthétique	
	cosmetic surgery
chirurgie (*f*) réparatrice	
	plastic surgery
coma (*m*)	*coma*
débrancher	*to switch off*
décéder#	*to die*
diagnostic (*m*)	*diagnosis*
douleur (*f*)	*pain*
effets (*mpl*) secondaires	*side effects*
enceinte	*pregnant*
s'évanouir	*to faint*
se faire# avorter	*to have an abortion*
fécondité (*f*)	*fertility*
frais (*mpl*) médicaux	
	medical expenses
guérir	*to cure*
guérison (*f*)	*cure*
handicapé/e (*m/f*)	
	handicapped person
incapacité (*f*)	*disability*

incurable	*incurable*
inéluctable	*inevitable*
infarctus (*m*)	*coronary*
insupportable	*unbearable*
intervention (*f*)chirurgicale	*operation*
invalidité (*f*)	*disability*
irréversible	*irreversible*
issue (*f*) fatale	*fatal outcome*
litige (*m*)	*lawsuit*
malentendants (*mpl*)	
	the hard of hearing
malin/maligne	*malignant*
médecine (*f*) douce	
	alternative medecine
non-voyants (*mpl*)	*the non-sighted*
pénible	*painful*
perfusion (*f*)	*intravenous drip*
pilule (*f*)	*pill*
pis-aller (*m*)	*last resort*
prise (*f*) de sang	*blood sample/test*
prothèse (*f*)	*artificial limb*
rechute (*f*)	*relapse*
salle (*f*) des urgences	
	emergency ward
Sécurité Sociale (*f*)	*Health Service*
soins (*mpl*) dentaires	*dental care*
souffrance (*f*)	*suffering*
sourd/e	*deaf*
stérilet (*m*)	*coil*
suicidaire (*m/f*)	
	person with suicidal tendencies
surmonter	*to overcome*
tranquillisant (*m*)	*tranquillizer*
trisomique (*m/f*)	
	Down's syndrome sufferer

un centre de dépistage anticancéreux	*cancer screening unit*
le service de traumatologie	*casualty department*
disposer de son corps comme on veut	*to do what one likes with one's body*
reprendre# conscience	*to regain consciousness*
le remède est pire que le mal	*the cure is worse than the disease*
ce médicament est remboursé par la Sécurité sociale	*the Health Service will reimburse you for the cost of this medicine*
le décès prématuré	*premature death*
le nombre de retraités va doubler	*the number of pensioners will double*
prolonger la vie	*to prolong life*
prendre# soin de sa santé	*to take care of one's health*
les pensions d'invalidité	*invalidity pensions*
la sédentarité	*sitting around every day*
les vaccinations en masse	*mass vaccinations*

SITES INTERNET UTILES

www.drogues.gouv.fr (site consacré aux drogues et aux toxicomanies)

www.chronodynamie.com/toxicaide/avenir.html (aides aux usagers de drogues)

www.apiweb.fr/toxicodependance/index.htm (forum de la toxicodépendance)

http://perso.wanadoo.fr/zanzan (site sur les méfaits des drogues)

www.ccsa.ca/cclat.htm (centre canadien de lutte contre l'alcoolisme et les toxicomanies)

www.alcoholics-anonymous.org/index_F.html (site des alcooliques anonymes)

www.sfa-ispa.ch/wwwispa/index_f.htm (institut suisse de prévention de l'alcoolisme et autres toxicomanies)

http://perso.wanadoo.fr/pascal.duhant/ (site personnel sur l'alcool)

www.pratique.fr/sante/aliment/index.html (site sur l'alimentation et diététique)

http://fr.dir.yahoo.com/Sante/Dietetique_et_nutrition/ (sites sur l'obésité et le végétarisme)

www.cdit.fr/actu_archives/archives.html (centre de documentation et d'information sur le tabac)

www.sidaweb.com/als.htm (association de lutte contre le SIDA)

www.information-jeunesse.tm.fr/ (des infos sur la santé, le SIDA etc)

www.survivants.org (site contre la contraception et l'avortement) http://svss-uspda.ch/factsfrek.htm (union suisse pour décriminaliser l'avortement)

www.droitdenaitre.org (site anti-avortement)

www.inserm.fr/ethique/Ethique.nsf (réseau d'info et de diffusion des connaissances en éthique médicale)

www.chu-rouen.fr/ssf/art/ethiquemedicale.html (sites francophones sur l'éthique médicale)

http://globegate.utm.edu/french/topics/medical.html (sites sur tous les aspects de la médecine)

www.prevention.ch (des infos sur la santé en Suisse)

http://hcsp.ensp.fr (haut comité de la santé publique)

http://www.sfsp-publichealth.org/ (la société française de santé publique)

www.sante.gouv.fr/index.htm (sites sur tous les aspects de la santé)

www.bruxelles-j.be/index.htm (site d'information jeunesse sur la santé)

www.club-internet.fr (infos sur la santé)

www.pratique.fr (sites sur la santé)

www.francealacarte.org.uk (le site du réseau culturel français au Royaume-Uni)

http://perso.wanadoo.fr/olivier-c/AnnuaireWeb.html (des adresses sur la santé)

LE TEMPS LIBRE

LES SPORTS

adepte (*m/f*)	*enthusiast*
s'adonner à	*to go in for*
adresse (*f*)	*skill*
aduler	*to hero-worship*
adversaire (*m/f*)	*opponent*
amateurisme (*m*)	*amateurism*
arbitre (*m*)	*referee, umpire*
attrait (*m*)	*appeal*
battre# le record	*to beat the record*
bien-être (*m*)	*well-being*
bienfaisant/e	*beneficial*
bienfait (*m*)	*benefit*
championnat (*m*)	*championship*
classement (*m*)	*rankings, standings*
compatriote (*m/f*)	
	fellow countryman/woman
concurrent/e (*m/f*)	*competitor*
se consacrer à	*to devote oneself to*
contrôle (*m*) anti-dopage	*drug check*
corrompu/e	*corrupt*
débutant/e (*m/f*)	*beginner*
défaite (*f*)	*loss*
se défouler	*to let off steam*
démotiver	*to demotivate*
détente (*f*)	*relaxation*
disqualifier	*to disqualify*
dopage (*m*)	*doping*
se doper	*to take drugs*
se dérouler	*to happen, to take place*

droitier/ière	*right-handed*
éliminatoire	*preliminary*
entraînement (*m*)	*training*
équipement (*m*)	*equipment*
esprit (*m*) d'équipe	*team spirit*
étape (*f*)	*lap, stage*
évacuer les tensions	
	to get rid of tension
événement (*m*) sportif	*sporting event*
exercice (*m*)	*exercise*
exploitation (*f*)	*exploitation*
fanatique (*m/f*)	*fan*
foule (*f*)	*crowd*
gagnant/e (*m/f*)	*winner*
gaucher/ère	*left-handed*
haute compétition (*f*)	
	top-level competition
huer	*to boo*
inconditionnel/le (*m/f*)	*enthusiast*
jeu (*m*) d'équipe	*team game*
se livrer à	*to devote oneself to*
ludique	*play (adj)*
maîtrise (*f*) de soi	*self-control*
maîtriser	*to master*
manche (*f*)	*round*
monnayer# son talent	
	to make money from one's talent
palme (*f*)	*prize*
passer professionnel	
	to turn professional
popularité (*f*)	*popularity*

pratiquant (*m*)	*player*
prélèvement (*m*) sanguin	*blood sample*
pratiquer	*to practise, to do*
prix (*m*) en argent (*m*)	*prize money*
rajeunir	*to make you feel younger*
randonnée (*f*)	*hike, walking*
rapprocher	*to bring together*
règles (*fpl*)	*rules*
remporter le titre	*to win the title*
rencontre (*f*)	*fixture*
roller (*m*)	*roller blades*
sain/e	*healthy*
spectateur/trice (*m/f*)	*spectator*
sport (*m*) collectif	*team sport*
sport (*m*) d'intérieur	*indoor sport*
sport (*m*) de masse	*very popular sport*
sport (*m*) de plein air	*outdoor sport*
sport (*m*) individuel	*individual sport*

sport-loisir (*m*)	*sport for all*
sportif/ve	*athletic*
sportivité (*f*)	*sportsmanship*
stage (*m*) de perfectionnement	*advanced training course*
substances (*fpl*) interdites	*banned substances*
succès (*m*)	*success*
se surpasser	*to excel oneself*
tactique (*f*)	*tactics*
toucher une prime	*to win a bonus*
tournoi (*m*)	*tournament*
transfert (*m*)	*transfer*
tricherie (*f*)	*cheating*
valorisation (*f*) de soi	*increase in self-esteem*
vedette (*f*) sportive	*sports star*
victoire (*f*)	*win*
vie (*f*) sédentaire	*inactive life*
vieillissement (*m*)	*growing old*

se livrer à une activité	*to involve oneself in an activity*
les stéroïdes anabolisants	*anabolic steroids*
détenir# le record mondial	*to hold the world record*
mélanger# le sport et la politique	*to mix sport and politics*
pour parvenir# au sommet	*to reach the top*
une carrière de courte durée	*a short-lived career*
se libérer# de son excès d'énergie	*to work off one's excess energy*
compromettre# sa santé	*to put one's health at risk*
décrocher une médaille/un record	*to win a medal/to set a record*
être contrôlé/e positif/positive	*to be tested positive*
prélever un échantillon d'urine	*to take a urine sample*
la cuillère de bois	*the wooden spoon*
les sportifs professionnels	*professional sportsmen and women*

LES PASSE-TEMPS

agréable	*enjoyable*
amitié (*f*)	*friendship*
autodidacte	*self-taught*
bénévolat (*m*)	*voluntary help*
boîte (*f*) de nuit	*night club*
bricolage (*m*)	*DIY*
casanier/ière	*stay-at-home*
centre (*m*) de loisirs	*leisure centre*
collectionner	*to collect*
cours (*m*) du soir	*evening class*
décompresser	*to unwind, relax*
délassement (*m*)	*relaxation*
distraction (*f*)	*amusement*
divertissement (*m*)	*relaxation, entertainment*
doué/e	*gifted*
engouement (*m*) pour	*craze for*

exceller à	*to excel at*
facultatif/ve	*optional*
foyer (*m*) des jeunes	*youth club*
gratifiant/e	*rewarding*
industrie (*f*) des loisirs	*entertainment industry*
installations (*fpl*)	*facilities*
s'inscrire# à	*to join*
s'intéresser à	*to be interested in*
intérêt (*m*)	*interest*
jardinage (*m*)	*gardening*
oisiveté (*f*)	*idleness*
parc (*m*) thématique	*theme park*
se passionner pour	*to be really keen on*
profiter de	*to take advantage of*
progrès (*mpl*) personnels	*self-improvement*
temps (*m*) libre	*free time*

la valorisation de soi	*increase in self-esteem*
à la portée de tout le monde	*accessible for everyone*
s'occuper l'esprit	*to keep one's mind active*
être# bien dans sa peau	*to feel happy and fulfilled*
la diminution du temps de travail	*the reduction in working hours*
les agréments de la vie	*the pleasures of life*
trouver du plaisir à faire quelque chose	*to derive enjoyment from doing something*
un passe-temps qui en vaut la peine	*a rewarding hobby*
les bonnes œuvres	*charitable works*
membre d'une association caritative	*member of a charitable organisation*
utiliser son temps à bon escient	*to use your time usefully*
développer ses talents	*to develop one's talents*

LE TOURISME

à ne pas manquer	*not to be missed*
accueil (*m*)	*welcome*
actif/ve	*active*
afflux (*m*)	*flood (of people)*
animé/e	*lively*
annulation (*f*)	*cancellation*
aoûtien/ne (*m/f*)	*August holiday-maker*
attrape-touristes (*m*)	*tourist trap*
aventureux/euse	*adventurous*
se baser à	*to be based in*
la belle saison	*summer months*
bronzage (*m*)	*suntan*
bronzage (*m*) intégral	*all-over tan*
circuit (*m*) touristique	*tourist circuit*
complexe (*m*) touristique	
	tourist complex
compliqué/e	*complicated*
croisière (*f*)	*cruise*
coutumes (*fpl*)	*habits, customs*
décalage (*m*) horaire	*time difference*
découverte (*f*)	*discovery*
déçu/e	*disappointed*
départ (*m*)	*departure*
déplacement (*m*)	*trip*
éloigné/e	*far off*
estival/e	*summer (adj)*
estivant/e (*m/f*)	*summer visitor*
étaler	*to stagger (holidays)*
évasion (*f*)	*escape*
explorer	*to explore*
faire# du tourisme	*to go sightseeing*

faire# étape	*to break the journey*
farniente (*m*)	*lazing around*
fin (*f*) de saison	*end of season*
folie (*f*)	*madness*
gîte (*m*)	*self-catering home*
guide (*m*) agréé	*qualified guide*
hébergement (*m*)	*accommodation*
hivernant/e (*m/f*)	*winter visitor*
industrie (*f*) du tourisme	
	tourist industry
inoubliable	*unforgettable*
juilletiste (*m/f*)	*July holiday-maker*
lieu (*m*) à la mode	*a fashionable place*
location (*f*)	*rent, hire*
lointain/e	*distant*
manière (*f*) de vivre	*way of life*
morte-saison (*f*)	*off-season*
nuitées (*fpl*)	*overnight stays*
paradis (*m*)	*paradise*
pittoresque	*picturesque*
propriété (*f*) à temps partagé	
	time-share flat
proximité (*f*)	*nearness*
récupérer	*to recover*
rentrée (*f*)	*return from holidays*
résidence (*f*) secondaire	*holiday home*
retour (*m*) à la nature	*back to nature*
réussi/e	*successful*
séjour (*m*) balnéaire	*seaside stay*
site (*m*)	*beauty spot*
station (*f*) de sports d'hiver	
	winter sports resort

station (f) familiale	*family resort*
tourisme (m) de masse	*mass tourism*
vacances (fpl) à thème	*special interest holidays*
vacancier/ière (m/f)	*holiday-maker*
valeur (f) éducative	*educational value*
vie (f) nocturne	*night life*
villégiature (f)	*holiday*
visite (f) d'échange	*exchange visit*
voyage (m) d'agrément	*pleasure trip*
voyage (m) organisé	*package holiday*
voyages (mpl)	*travelling*
weekend (m) prolongé	*extended weekend*

faire# le pont	*to make a long weekend of it*
les vacances de Pâques ont lieu tôt cette année	*the Easter holidays fall early this year*
le premier pays touristique du monde	*the world's number one tourist destination*
la formule du soleil, sable et sexe reste populaire	*sun, sand and sex remains a popular recipe*
élargir ses horizons	*to broaden one's outlook*
avoir# envie de voir le monde	*to have the travel bug*
aller# à la recherche du soleil	*to go in search of some sun*
pour faire# face au déferlement de vacanciers	*to cope with the flood of holidaymakers*
les vacances, c'est la soupape de sécurité	*holidays are a safety valve*
estamper les touristes	*to fleece the tourists*
l'exode de Paris	*the mass departure from Paris*
dégagé/e des contraintes quotidiennes	*away from the daily grind*
rayonner dans une région	*to tour around an area from a base*
favoriser l'entente entre les pays	*to further understanding between countries*
avoir# une valeur éducative	*to be of educational value*
recharger# les batteries	*to recharge one's batteries*
les devises étrangères	*foreign currency*

SITES INTERNET UTILES

www.lokace.com (des sites sur les sports et le tourisme)

http://globegate.utm.edu/french/globegate_mirror/sport.html (sports et loisirs en Francophonie)

www.club-internet.fr/selection/sport_loisir/ (des infos sur les sports et les loisirs) www.jeunesse-sports.gouv.fr/mjshome.htm (ministère de la jeunesse et des sports)

www.cplus.fr/html/sports/sports.htm (Canal Plus - les actualités sur le sport)

www.multimania.com/05/zazou (le dopage dans les sports)

www.information-jeunesse.tm.fr/ (des infos sur les sports et les loisirs)

www.grolier.fr/studio (des infos sur le sport et le tourisme)

http://perso.wanadoo.fr/olivier-c/AnnuaireWeb.html (des adresses sur le sport et le tourisme)

www.club-internet.fr/voyages (des infos sur les voyages)

www.franceguide.com/fr/france.htm (les séjours en France)

www.bordeaux-tourisme.com/ (le tourisme à Bordeaux)

www.club-internet.fr/ (des infos sur les voyages)

www.ambafrance.org/LINKS/ (sites sur le tourisme et les loisirs)

www.bruxelles-j.be/fichinfo_fs.htm (des fiches sur les loisirs et les vacances)

www.voyage.fr (site sur les voyages)

UN TOUR DU MONDE

LA GUERRE ET LA PAIX

abri (*m*)	*shelter*
aides (*fpl*) humanitaires	*humanitarian aid*
alliés (*mpl*)	*allies*
ancien combattant (*m*)	*war veteran*
armée (*f*) de métier	*professional army*
armes (*fpl*) chimiques	*chemical weapons*
aviation (*f*) coalisée	*allied aircraft*
aviation (*f*) de combat	*fighter force*
blocus (*m*)	*blockade*
bouclier (*m*) humain	*human shield*
camp (*m*) de réfugiés	*refugee camp*
capituler	*to surrender*
cessez-le-feu (*m*)	*ceasefire*
combats (*mpl*) acharnés	*heavy fighting*
conférence (*f*) de paix	*peace conference*
conflit (*m*)	*conflict*
conquérir#	*to conquer*
contrôle (*m*) des armements	*arms control*
convoi (*m*) humanitaire	*humanitarian convoy*
course (*f*) à l'armement	*arms race*
criminel (*m*) de guerre	*war criminal*
défaite (*f*)	*defeat*
désarmement (*m*) unilatéral	*unilateral disarmament*
détestable	*appalling*
dommages (*mpl*) collatéraux	*collateral damage*
effectuer un raid	*to carry out a raid*
embargo (*m*)	*embargo*
s'emparer de	*to seize*
en guerre	*at war*
engager#	*to enlist*
entre-deux-guerres (*m*)	*inter-war years*
envahir	*to invade*
escalade (*f*)	*escalation*
état (*m*) des pertes	*casualty list*
évacuer	*to evacuate*
éviter	*to avoid*
fabricant (*m*) d'armes	*arms manufacturer*
faire# la guerre à	*to wage war on*
force (*f*) de frappe	*strike force*
forces (*fpl*) armées	*armed forces*
frappe (*f*) aérienne	*air strike*
fusée (*f*)	*rocket*
guerre (*f*) chimique	*chemical warfare*
guerre (*f*) civile	*civil war*
guerre (*f*) d'embuscade	*guerrilla warfare*
guerre (*f*) mondiale	*world war*

guerre (*f*) nucléaire	*nuclear war*
haine (*f*)	*hatred*
hélicoptère (*m*) de combat	*helicopter gunship*
initiative (*f*) de paix	*peace initiative*
intervenir	*to intervene*
lancer#	*to launch*
manifestation (*f*) pacifiste	*peace march*
manœuvres (*fpl*)	*manoeuvres*
mater	*to subdue, quell*
matériel (*m*) de guerre	*weaponry*
mines (*fpl*) antipersonnel	*anti-personnel mines*
missile (*m*) à longue portée	*long-range missile*
mutilés (*mpl*) de guerre	*war-disabled*
neutre	*neutral*
objecteur (*m*) de conscience	*conscientious objector*
ogive (*f*) nucléaire	*nuclear warhead*

pacifique	*peaceful, peace-loving*
pacifiste (*m/f*)	*pacifist*
paix (*f*)	*peace*
population (*f*) civile	*civilian population*
porte-avions (*m*)	*aircraft carrier*
pourparlers (*mpl*) de paix	*peace talks*
prendre# d'assaut	*to take by storm*
préventif/ve	*pre-emptive*
prisonnier (*m*) de guerre	*prisoner of war*
prolifération (*f*) nucléaire	*nuclear proliferation*
purification (*f*) ethnique	*ethnic cleansing*
réfugiés (*mpl*)	*refugees*
service (*m*) militaire	*military service*
solution (*f*) négociée	*negotiated settlement*
superpuissances (*fpl*)	*super-powers*
trêve (*f*)	*truce*
troupes (*fpl*) terrestres	*ground forces*

déchiré/e par la guerre	*war-torn*
recourir# à la force	*to resort to force*
être# dans une position de force	*to be in a position of strength*
la force de dissuasion nucléaire	*the nuclear deterrent*
les forces de maintien de la paix	*peace-keeping forces*
un pays détenteur d'armes nucléaires	*a country which possesses nuclear weapons*
la raison du plus fort est toujours la meilleure	*might is right*
vivre# dans la peur d'une nouvelle guerre	*to live in fear of another war*
il y a eu de nombreuses victimes	*there were heavy casualties*

la guerre dans toute sa laideur	*the full horror of war*
appliquer des sanctions économiques	*to apply economic sanctions*
faire# son service militaire	*to do one's military service*
déclencher une guerre	*to trigger off a war*
commettre# des atrocités	*to commit atrocities*
les relations diplomatiques	*diplomatic relations*
signer un accord de paix	*to sign a peace agreement*
maintenir# la paix	*to keep the peace*
débloquer la situation	*to get things moving again*
des crimes contre l'humanité	*crimes against humanity*
lâcher des bombes	*to drop bombs*
prendre# le dessus	*to gain the upper hand*

LA RELIGION

adepte (*m/f*)	*follower*
adorer	*to worship*
s'agenouiller	*to kneel (down)*
agnostique (*m/f*)	*agnostic*
aller# à l'église	*to go to church*
âme (*f*)	*soul*
ange (*m*)	*angel*
assistance (*f*)	*congregation*
astrologie (*f*)	*astrology*
athée (*m/f*)	*atheist*
athéisme (*m*)	*atheism*
au-delà (*m*)	*afterworld*
autel (*m*)	*altar*
baptême (*m*)	*baptism*
bénir	*to bless*
Bible (*f*)	*Bible*
Bouddhisme (*m*)	*Buddhism*
Carême (*m*)	*Lent*
catholicisme (*m*)	*Catholicism*
cérémonie (*f*)	*ceremony*
chaire (*f*)	*pulpit*
chrétien/ne (*m/f*)	*Christian*
christianiser	*to convert to Christianity*
christianisme (*m*)	*Christianity*
ciel (*m*)	*heaven*
communier	*to receive communion*
convertir à	*to convert to*
Coran (*m*)	*Koran*
croire# en Dieu	*to believe in God*
croix (*f*)	*cross*
croyances (*fpl*) religieuses	*religious beliefs*
croyant/e (*m/f*)	*believer*
culte (*m*)	*worship*
diable (*m*)	*devil*
Église (*f*) orthodoxe	*Orthodox Church*
enfer (*m*)	*hell*

espoir (*m*)	*hope*
évangéliste (*m/f*)	
	born-again Christian
évêque (*m*)	*bishop*
extrémisme (*m*) islamique	
	islamic extremism
fidèles (*mpl*)	*the faithful*
foi (*f*)	*faith*
fondateur (*m*)	*founder*
gourou (*m*)	*guru*
groupe (*m*) islamiste	*Islamic group*
immortalité (*f*)	*immortality*
intégriste (*m/f*)	*fundamentalist*
islam (*m*)	*Islam*
jeûne (*m*) du Ramadan	
	fast of Ramadan
jour (*m*) du seigneur	*the Lord's Day*
juif/juive (*m/f*)	*Jew*
matérialisme (*m*)	*materialism*
Mecque (*f*)	*Mecca*
méditer	*to meditate*
messe (*f*)	*mass*
Messie (*m*)	*Messiah*
mœurs (*fpl*)	*morals*
moine (*m*)	*monk*
mosquée (*f*)	*mosque*
musulman/e (*m/f*)	*Muslim*
nirvâna (*m*)	*nirvana*
nourriture (*f*) kascher	*kosher food*
office (*m*) religieux	*service*
pape (*m*)	*Pope*
paroisse (*f*)	*parish*

pécheur/pécheresse (*m/f*)	*sinner*
péché (*m*)	*sin*
pèlerinage (*m*)	*pilgrimage*
peuple (*m*) élu	*chosen people*
port (*m*) du voile	*wearing a veil*
position (*f*) du lotus	
	the lotus position
pratiquant/e (*m/f*)	*churchgoer*
prêcher	*to preach*
prédication (*f*)	*preaching, sermon*
présent (*m*)	*the here and now*
prière (*f*)	*prayer*
profane	*secular*
prophète (*m*)	*prophet*
rabbin (*m*)	*rabbi*
réconforter	*to comfort*
religieuse (*f*)	*nun*
sacerdotal	*priestly*
saint (*m*) suaire	*Holy Shroud*
Saint-Esprit (*m*)	*Holy Spirit*
Sainte Vierge (*f*)	*Virgin Mary*
salut (*m*)	*salvation*
secte (*f*)	*sect*
sens (*m*) de la vie	*meaning of life*
souffrance (*f*)	*suffering*
superstition (*f*)	*superstition*
synagogue (*f*)	*synagogue*
système (*m*) de valeurs	
	system of values
Témoin (*m*) de Jéhovah	
	Jehovah's witness
vaudou (*m*)	*voodoo*

l'infaillibilité pontificale	*papal infallibility*
croire# à la vie après la mort	*to believe in life after death*
être# enseveli/e/enterré(e) chrétiennement	*to have a Christian burial*
prier Dieu de faire un miracle	*to pray for a miracle*
il n'est plus pratiquant	*he doesn't go to church any more*
un catholique qui n'est plus pratiquant	*a lapsed Catholic*
la poussée de l'Islam	*the upsurge of Islam*
se détourner de la religion	*to turn away from religion*
la prise de position morale de l'Église	*the Church's moral standpoint*
la méditation transcendantale	*transcendental meditation*
abandonner le culte	*to give up one's religion*
se tourner vers la religion	*to turn to religion*
le Christ ressuscité	*the risen Christ*
la recherche des satisfactions non matérielles	*the search for non material satisfaction*

LE TIERS-MONDE

affamé/e	*starving*
agoniser	*to be dying*
aide (*f*) alimentaire	*food aid*
aide (*f*) au développement	*development aid*
aide (*f*) étrangère	*foreign aid*
aide (*f*) humanitaire	*humanitarian aid*
aide (*f*) liée	*tied aid*
alléger#	*to lessen, to relieve*
analphabétisme (*m*)	*illiteracy*
s'appauvrir	*to grow poorer*
bidonville (*m*)	*shanty town*
ciblé(e) sur	*targeted at*
corruption (*f*)	*corruption*
crise (*f*)	*crisis*
défavorisé/e	*underprivileged*
denrées (*fpl*)	*food supplies*
dénué/e de tout	*destitute*
déshérité/e	*deprived*
disette (*f*)	*food shortage*
durable	*lasting*
eau (*f*) potable	*drinking water*
endetté/e	*in debt*
espérance (*f*) de vie	*life expectancy*
exploiter	*to exploit*
illettré/e	*illiterate*
impuissant/e	*powerless*
inégalité (*f*)	*inequality*
installations (*fpl*) sanitaires	*sanitation*
insuffisant/e	*inadequate*
irriguer	*to irrigate*

les moins nantis	*the less well-off*
maladie (*f*)	*disease*
malédiction (*f*)	*curse*
malnutrition (*f*) aiguë	*chronic malnutrition*
matières (*fpl*) premières	*raw materials*
mendier	*to beg (for)*
mousson (*f*)	*monsoon*
Occident (*m*)	*the West*
octroyer# de l'aide	*to grant aid*
opprimé/e	*oppressed*
paludisme (*m*)	*malaria*
pays (*m*) donateur	*donor country*
pays (*m*) industrialisé	*industrialised country*
pays (*mpl*) occidentaux	*western countries*

piller	*to pillage*
régime (*m*) corrompu	*corrupt regime*
régulation (*f*) des naissances	*birth control*
retard (*m*) économique	*economic backwardness*
société (*f*) de secours	*relief organisation*
sort (*m*)	*fate*
souffrance (*f*)	*suffering*
sous-alimenté/e	*under-nourished*
sous-développé/e	*under-developed*
surexploitation (*f*)	*over-exploitation*
surpopulation (*f*)	*over-population*
suspension (*f*) de l'aide	*suspension of aid*
taudis (*m*)	*slum*
taux (*m*) de mortalité	*mortality rate*

lancer# un appel aux pays riches	*to appeal to the rich countries*
s'atteler# à promouvoir le développement	*to get down to promoting development*
le soulagement de la misère	*the relief of poverty*
l'alphabétisation de la population	*teaching people to read and write*
financer# des programmes de développement	*to finance development programmes*
un pays en voie de développement	*developing country*
parrainer un enfant	*to sponsor a child*
l'espoir d'un avenir meilleur	*the hope of a better future*
privilégier# la santé	*to give greater importance to health*
laisser le pays exsangue	*to bleed the country dry*
un représentant d'un organisme humanitaire	*aid-worker*
alléger# la souffrance	*to relieve suffering*

se tirer de la misère par leurs propres efforts	*to escape poverty by their own efforts*
le droit des peuples à se nourrir eux-mêmes	*the right of nations to feed themselves*
la nourriture n'atteint pas ceux qui en ont besoin	*food does not reach those in need of it*
le taux de mortalité infantile	*children's death rate*
un faible taux d'espérance de vie	*a short life expectancy*
un enfant qui ne pèse pas assez	*an underweight child*
souffrir# de malnutrition	*to suffer from malnutrition*
annuler les dettes	*to cancel the debts*
le fossé informatique et économique	*the digital and economic divide*

LES CATASTROPHES

abattre#	*to knock down*
s'affaisser	*to collapse, to give way*
affligé/e	*distressed*
anéantir	*to annihilate*
angoisse (*f*)	*distress*
arracher	*to uproot*
atteint/e	*affected*
avertissement (*m*)	*warning*
boîte (*f*) noire	*black box*
brasier (*m*)	*inferno*
broyer#	*to crush*
cadavre (*m*)	*corpse*
calciné/e	*charred, burnt to a cinder*
carambolage (*m*)	*pile-up*
catastrophe (*f*) naturelle	*natural disaster*
cauchemar (*m*)	*nightmare*
chapelle (*f*) ardente	*chapel of rest*
condoléances (*fpl*)	*sympathy*

coulée (*f*) de boue	*mud slide*
couler	*to sink*
coupure (*f*) de courant	*power cut*
déblayage (*m*)	*clearing up*
décombres (*mpl*)	*debris, rubble*
déflagration (*f*)	*explosion*
défoncer#	*to smash in*
dégager#	*to free*
dégâts (*mpl*)	*damage*
destructeur/trice	*destructive*
détruire#	*to destroy*
deuil (*m*)	*mourning*
dévastateur/trice	*devastating*
dévasté/e	*devastated*
diluvien/ne	*torrential*
disette (*f*)	*food shortage*
écraser	*to squash*
s'écraser	*to crash*
s'effondrer	*to collapse*
ensevelir	*to bury*

épauler	*to back up, support*	repêcher	*to recover (bodies)*
épave (*f*)	*wreck*	rescapé/e (*m/f*)	*survivor*
erreur (*f*) humaine	*human error*	rude	*harsh, severe*
éruption (*f*)	*outbreak*	sain/e et sauf/ve	*safe and sound*
évacuer	*to evacuate*	sanglant/e	*bloody*
exploser	*to explode*	sauvetage (*m*)	*rescue*
funèbre	*gloomy, dismal*	sauveteur (*m*)	*rescuer*
gravats (*mpl*)	*rubble (small pieces)*	sécheresse (*f*)	*drought*
grièvement	*seriously*	secousse (*f*)	*shock*
heurter	*to strike*	séisme (*m*)	*earthquake*
hospitaliser	*to take to hospital*	sinistre (*m*)	*disaster*
incendie (*m*)	*fire*	sinistré/e	*disaster-stricken*
indemne	*unhurt*	sinistré/e (*m/f*)	*disaster victim*
inondation (*f*)	*flood*	sombrer	*to sink*
naufrage (*m*)	*shipwreck*	touché/e par	*affected by*
navrant/e	*heartbreaking*	tragédie (*f*)	*tragedy*
percuter (contre)	*to crash into*	tremblement (*m*) de terre	*earthquake*
périr	*to perish*	victime (*f*)	*victim*
ravager#	*to devastate*	vivant/e	*alive*
règles (*fpl*) de sécurité	*safety rules*	zone (*f*) sinistrée	*disaster area*

provoquer la mort de trois personnes	*to cause the death of three people*
d'après les derniers chiffres	*according to the latest figures*
évaluer le montant des dégâts	*to work out the total amount of damage*
le vent attise les feux	*the wind is fanning the flames*
dépêcher sur les lieux	*to dispatch to the scene*
travailler sans relâche	*to work non-stop*
lancer# un appel d'urgence	*to launch an emergency appeal*
déclarer l'état d'urgence	*to declare a state of emergency*
le bilan provisoire	*the provisional death-toll*
le bilan définitif	*the final death-toll*
ravagé/e par la famine	*laid waste by famine*

L'UE

adhérer# à	to belong to
affecter des crédits	to allocate funds
barrière (f) douanière	customs barrier
bureaucratie (f)	bureaucracy
céder#	to give way
clause (f) d'exemption	opt-out clause
communauté (f)	community
convertir	to convert
député (m) européen	Euro MP
eurocrate (m/f)	Eurocrat (EU employee)
l'européisme (m)	europeanism
eurosceptique (m/f)	eurosceptic
fédéral/e	federal
frontalier/ière	border (adj)
libre circulation (f)	freedom of movement
Marché (m) commun	Common Market
marché (m) unique	single market
monnaie (f) unique	single currency
négocier	to negotiate
parlement (m) européen	European Parliament
passer la frontière	to cross the border
pays (m) membre	member country
pays (m) voisin	neighbouring country
présidence (f)	presidency
protectionnisme (m)	protectionism
ressortissant/e (m/f)	citizen
sigle (m) de l'euro	the Euro symbol
souveraineté (f)	sovereignty
subventionner	to subsidise
traité (m)	treaty
transfrontalier/ière	cross-border
union (f) européenne	European Union
union (f) monétaire	monetary union
vote (m) majoritaire	majority voting
zone (f) euro	the Euro zone

la libre circulation des travailleurs	free movement of labour
la politique agricole commune	Common Agricultural Policy
respecter les directives de l'UE	to follow EU directives
les règlements de l'UE	EU regulations
l'harmonisation communautaire	community-wide standardisation
être# profondément divisé/e par	to be deeply divided by
rendre# la Communauté plus apte à	to make the Community more capable of
l'élargissement de la Communauté	widening the Community
renforcer# le sentiment européen	to strengthen European feeling
concerter l'action	to act together
craindre# la perte de l'identité nationale	to fear the loss of national identity
se montrer très européen/ne	to be pro-European

la monnaie est en danger	*the currency is under threat*
l'Europe à deux vitesses	*two speed Europe*
l'adhésion à l'UE	*membership of the European Union*
organiser un référendum	*to hold a referendum*
un euro vaut …	*one euro is worth …*
rater le coche	*to miss the boat*
l'hostilité envers l'Europe	*hostility towards Europe*
une Europe de plus en plus intégrée	*an increasingly integrated Europe*
craindre# de perdre son identité nationale	*to fear losing one's national identity*

LE LOGEMENT

agent (*m*) immobilier	*estate agent*
aménager	*to convert*
ameublement (*m*)	*furnishing*
bail (*m*)	*lease*
bâtir	*to build*
béton (*m*)	*concrete*
chantier (*m*)	*building-site*
construire#	*to construct, build*
crise (*f*) du logement	*housing shortage*
délabré/e	*dilapidated*
déménager#	*to move house*
domicile (*m*)	*home, residence*
emménager#	*to move in*
facture (*f*) de gaz	*gas bill*
foncier/ière	*land (adj)*
habitat (*m*)	*housing conditions*
immeuble (*m*)	*block of flats*
immobilier (*m*)	*property business*
industrie (*f*) du bâtiment	*building industry*
insalubre	*unhealthy*

locataire (*m/f*)	*tenant*
maison-modèle (*f*)	*show house*
malsain/e	*unhealthy*
mètre (*m*) carré	*square metre*
meublé/e	*furnished*
non-meublé/e	*unfurnished*
occupant (*m*) propriétaire	*owner-occupier*
pénurie (*f*)	*shortage*
propriété (*f*)	*property*
réhabiliter	*to restore*
relogement (*m*)	*rehousing*
rénovation (*f*)	*renovation*
résidence (*f*) principale	*main home*
résidence (*f*) secondaire	*holiday home*
retaper	*to do up*
spacieux/euse	*roomy*
squatter	*to squat*
statut (*m*) social	*social status*
taudis (*m*)	*slum*
taxe (*f*) d'habitation	*council tax*
terrain (*m*)	*building plot*
vétuste	*old and dilapidated*

les conditions de vie	*living conditions*
la contrainte économique	*economic constraint*
un cadre de vie	*a living environment*
les familles à revenu moyen	*families on average income*
l'urbanisation sauvage	*unplanned building*
le placement pierre	*investment in bricks and mortar*
charbonnier est maître dans sa maison	*you are master in your own home*
être# propriétaire	*to be a home-owner*
la France profonde	*the broad mass of French people*
les logements sociaux	*council homes*

EN VILLE

agglomération (*f*)	*built-up area*
aire (*f*) de jeux	*adventure playground*
aménagement (*m*) piétonnier	*pedestrianisation*
animation (*f*)	*bustle*
anonymat (*m*)	*anonymity*
arrondissement (*m*)	*district*
attrayant/e	*attractive, appealing*
banlieue (*f*)	*suburb*
banlieusard/e (*m/f*)	*commuter*
bitume (*m*)	*asphalt*
brouhaha (*m*)	*hubbub*
cadre (*m*)	*setting*
ceinture (*f*) verte	*green belt*
citadin/e (*m/f*)	*city dweller*
cité (*f*)	*estate*
cité (*f*) ouvrière	*housing estate*
ensemble (*m*) immobilier	*housing scheme*
s'entasser	*to cram together*
espace (*m*) vert	*green space, park*
faire# la navette	*to commute*
faubourg (*m*)	*inner suburb*
fond (*m*) sonore	*background noise*
gratte-ciel (*m*)	*skyscraper*
HLM (*f*)	*council flat*
labyrinthe (*m*)	*maze, rabbit-warren*
laideur (*f*)	*ugliness*
loyer (*m*)	*rent*
mobilier (*m*) urbain	*street furniture*
périphérique	*outlying*
pôle (*m*) urbain	*urban centre*
prospère	*prosperous*
quartier (*m*)	*neighbourhood*
quartier (*m*) résidentiel	*residential area*
repeupler	*to repopulate*
se ressembler	*to look alike*
rues (*fpl*) piétonnes	*pedestrianised streets*
sans âme (*f*)	*soulless*

services (*mpl*) publics	*public services*
sortie (*f*) de la ville	*edge of town*
stressé/e	*stressful*
surpeuplé/e	*overcrowded*
terrain (*m*) vague	*waste ground*
trépidant/e	*hectic*
tristesse (*f*)	*sadness*
s'urbaniser	*to become built-up*

urbanisme (*m*)	*town planning*
urbaniste (*m*)	*town planner*
ville (*f*) satellite	*satellite town*
ville-dortoir (*f*)	*dormitory town*
voisinage (*m*)	*neighbourhood*
zone (*f*) d'activités	*business park*
zone (*f*) piétonnière	
	pedestrian precinct

la densité de population	*population density*
faire# partie du charme de la ville	*to be part of the charm of the town*
la situation dans les banlieues à problèmes est intenable	*the situation in the problem suburbs is intolerable*
une ville sans agrément	*an unattractive town*
situé/e dans un cadre de verdure	*in a leafy setting*
la dégradation du cadre de vie	*the worsening of the environment*
un quartier laissé à l'abandon	*a run-down area*
rendre les villes plus vivables	*to make towns more pleasant to live in*
embellir le cadre urbain	*to smarten up the town environment*
l'insécurité des grandes villes	*the lack of safety in the cities*

À LA CAMPAGNE

abords (*mpl*)	*surroundings*
agrément (*m*)	*charm*
alentours (*mpl*)	
	surroundings, vicinity
ambiance (*f*)	*atmosphere*
calme (*m*)	*calm*
campagnard/e (*m/f*)	*country dweller*
commérages (*mpl*)	*gossip*
communauté (*f*)	*community*
commune (*f*)	*district*

décroître#	*to decrease*
dépaysement (*m*)	*disorientation*
dépeuplement (*m*)	*depopulation*
éloignement (*m*)	*distance*
endormi/e	*sleepy*
équipements (*mpl*)	*facilities*
exode (*m*) rural	*drift from the land*
idyllique	*idyllic*
s'implanter	*to settle*
infrastructure (*f*)	*infrastructure*
isolé/e	*cut off, isolated*

mieux-vivre (*m*)		région (*f*) arriérée	*backward area*
	improved standard of living	reposant/e	*restful*
mode (*m*) de vie	*way of life*	rural/e	*rural*
mythe (*m*)	*myth*	site (*m*) protégé	*preservation area*
nature (*f*)	*nature*	survie (*f*) du village	
paisible	*peaceful*		*survival of the village*
pittoresque	*picturesque*	verdure (*f*)	*greenery*
recensement (*m*)	*census*	vie (*f*) villageoise	*village life*

faire# quelque chose à son rythme	*to do something at one's own pace*
jouir de la paix	*to enjoy the peace*
s'exiler à la campagne	*to bury oneself in the country*
les changements survenus dans l'agriculture	*changes that have come about in agriculture*
la campagne dépeuplée	*the deserted countryside*
les charmes de la vie à la campagne	*the attractions of country life*

SITES INTERNET UTILES

www.historial.org (histoire de la Grande Guerre)

www.ifrance.com/historia (la seconde guerre mondiale jour après jour)

http://members.aol.com/historel/index.htm (l'histoire des religions)

www.religion.qc.ca (centre de consultation sur les nouvelles religions)

http://perso.wanadoo.fr/olivier-c/AnnuaireWeb.html (des adresses sur la religion)

www.globenet.org/ritimo/cdtm75/ (centre de documentation Tiers Monde de Paris)

www.paris.msf.org/ (site des médecins sans frontières)

www.un.org/french (site des Nations Unies)

www.amnesty.asso.fr/index_home.htm (section française d'Amnesty International)

www.medecinsdumonde.org (site de l'organisation 'Médecins du Monde')

www.prevention2000.org/cat_nat/index1.htm (site sur les catastrophes naturelles)

www.multimania.com/voutay/meteo/meteo.html (site sur les catastrophes météorologiques) http://perso.wanadoo.fr/medilor (association humanitaire)

www.aui-ong.org (site de l'action d'urgence internationale)

www.francealacarte.org.uk (le site du réseau culturel français au Royaume-Uni)

www.erm.lu/epm/index.htm (le magazine du Parlement et de l'actualité européenne)

http://ue.eu.int/fr/summ.htm (le conseil de l'Union Européenne)

www.bruxelles-j.be/index.htm (site d'information jeunesse sur le logement)

www.pratique.fr (sites sur le logement)

www.grame.qc.ca/me.enc.html (la ville plus attrayante que la banlieue?)

http:///www.equipement.gouv.fr/urbanisme (centre de documentation de l'urbanisme)

www.village.tm.fr/Index.htm (site sur la vie à la campagne)

www.fnau.org (fédération nationale des Agences d'Urbanisme)

CONCLUSION

LES PHRASES

1 Essays usually deal with problems or topics of concern, and the introduction to an essay tries to place these in context:

un problème qui touche toutes les couches sociales
a problem that affects all levels of society

ce problème est au premier plan de nos préoccupations
this problem is uppermost in our minds

un thème brûlant de l'actualité *a burning issue of the moment*

un problème fort difficile à résoudre *a very difficult problem to solve*

une question qui provoque bien des controverses
a question that causes a great deal of controversy

ce problème a été rendu plus aigu par *this problem has been made more acute by*

le coût social est astronomique *the social cost is astronomical*

un problème dont il est souvent question *a recurring problem*

l'importance de ce phénomène ne peut être sous-estimée
the importance of this phenomenon cannot be over-stated

une des plus grandes menaces qui pèsent sur le monde
one of the biggest threats facing the world

tout est en train de se transformer en profondeur, à un rythme accéléré
everything is changing vastly, at a quickening pace

le problème a pris une telle ampleur que *the problem has reached such proportions that*

le point de non-retour est dépassé *the point of no-return has been passed*

les événements prennent une tournure tragique
events are taking a tragic turn for the worse

la situation ne cesse de se dégrader *the situation keeps getting worse*

les origines du problème résident dans *the roots of the problem lie in*

nous vivons dans un monde où *we live in a world where*

le problème est beaucoup plus sérieux qu'on ne se l'imagine
the problem is much more serious than people think

au début du troisième millénaire *at the start of the third millennium*

nous vivons une période de grandes mutations *we are living at a time of great change*

avoir# une portée mondiale *to have a world-wide effect*

2 Introductions should indicate the course that the essay will take:

cette dissertation a pour but de   *this essay aims to*

j'ai pour objet de présenter et d'analyser les faits

        my aim is to present and analyse the facts

pour avoir une vision plus précise de la situation

        to obtain a clearer picture of the position

on va examiner les avantages et les inconvénients de

        we shall examine the advantages and the disadvantages of

j'essaierai de déterminer les causes principales de

        I shall try to determine the main causes of

il faut d'abord définir les idées clés, c'est-à-dire

        the key ideas must first of all be defined, namely

3 A paragraph may usefully begin or end with a rhetorical question, to which a suggested answer is then provided:

comment, alors, traiter le problème de... ?	*how then shall we deal with the problem of... ?*
comment inverser cette tendance?	*how can we reverse this trend?*
peut-on remédier aux difficultés de... ?	*can we put right the difficulties of... ?*
est-il possible de généraliser?	*is it possible to generalise?*
quelles solutions pourrait-on envisager?	*what solutions might be borne in mind?*
est-ce qu'on peut dire que... ?	*can we say that ... ?*
de quoi s'agit-il en fait?	*what in fact is at issue?*
tout dépend-il de... ?	*does everything depend on ... ?*
comment aborder un problème qui... ?	*how can we tackle a problem that ... ?*
dans quelle mesure peut-on attribuer... ?	*how far can we attribute ... ?*

4 Phrases to start off a paragraph in the main body of the essay could include:

en guise d'introduction	*by way of an introduction*
réfléchissons d'abord à	*let's first consider*
pour approfondir la question	*to go into the matter in more depth*
dans l'état actuel des choses	*the way things stand at the moment*
il faut en venir maintenant à	*we must now turn to*
comme point de départ on pourrait	*as a starting point we could*
l'une des conséquences les plus évidentes est	*one of the most obvious consequences is*
un autre aspect du problème est que	*another side of the problem is*
sur le plan humain, il faut considérer	*on a human level we must consider*
pour commencer, il serait utile de	*to start off it would be useful to*
une des premières questions qui se posent	*one of the first questions that arises*

en ce qui concerne	*as far as ... is concerned*
il faut également mentionner	*mention must also be made of*
en premier lieu examinons	*to start off with let's examine*
pour tirer l'affaire au clair	*to clarify the matter*

5 Ideas about how to solve the problem may well be put forward:

le problème ne peut être traité qu'au niveau de	*the problem can only be dealt with at the level of*
il faut mener une action d'envergure nationale	*we must take action on a national scale*
l'autre solution est de	*the other solution is to*
la clé du problème est	*the key to the problem is*
pour que ce fléau cesse de s'étendre, il faut	*to stop this scourge spreading we must*
mettre sur pied un système au moyen duquel on peut	*to set up a system whereby we can*
ce ne serait pas une mauvaise idée de	*it wouldn't be a bad idea to*
on pourrait envisager de	*we could contemplate*
ceci est sans doute dû en partie à	*this is no doubt partly due to the fact that*
une solution facile qui s'impose	*one vital, easy solution*
ce problème tire ses origines dans	*this problem has its roots in*

6 You may wish to show your or other people's strong views about the topic:

il est scandaleux de	*it is scandalous to*
il serait abusif de	*it would be putting it a bit strongly to*
il n'est pas question de	*it's not a matter of*
ce serait de la folie de	*it would be madness to*
c'est une politique vouée à l'échec	*it's a policy that is bound to fail*
contrairement à ce que l'on croit généralement	*contrary to popular belief*
ce qu'il y a de certain, c'est que	*what is certain is that*
il est fortement déconseillé de	*it is highly inadvisable to*
la société ne peut pas tolérer	*society cannot tolerate*
il est hors de question que	*it's out of the question that*
il ne fait aucun doute que	*there's no doubt that*
on exagérerait à peine en disant que	*it would scarcely be an exaggeration to say that*
la vérité est que	*the fact of the matter is that*
il importe de comprendre que	*it is vital to realise that*
il faut s'élever contre	*one must object to*
il ne saurait être question de	*there can be no question of*
le facteur le plus important est que	*the most important factor is that*

loin de résoudre le problème, cela pourrait	*far from solving the problem, that could*
cette ligne de conduite court le risque de	*this course of action runs the risk of*
on ne peut manquer d'être frappé par	*one cannot help but be struck by*
nous vivons dans un État «nounou» où…	*we live in a nanny state where…*

7 It may be that you know what needs to be done:

cela aurait pour conséquence de	*that would have the result of*
entamer des mesures concrètes	*to initiate concrete measures*
il incombe au gouvernement de	*it is up to the government to*
il conviendrait de	*it would be right to*
une mesure d'importance primordiale	*a step of supreme importance*
pour résoudre les problèmes soulevés, il faut	*to solve the problems raised it is necessary to*

8 Of course, you may not have clear-cut ideas or solutions:

il n'est pas aisé de se forger une opinion	*it isn't easy to form a clear opinion*
certains soutiennent que	*some people maintain that*
les avis sont partagés sur	*opinions are divided over*
il est à prévoir que	*the likely outcome is that*
il reste à savoir si	*it remains to be seen whether*
on voit mal comment	*it is hard to see how*
il pourrait y avoir	*there could well be*
tout semble indiquer que	*everything seems to point to the fact that*
il est difficile de ne pas succomber à	*it's hard not to give in to*
personne n'a réussi à trouver la solution miracle	*nobody has yet come up with the miracle solution*
il ne faut pas s'attendre à une percée spectaculaire	*we cannot expect a spectacular breakthrough*
il est illusoire de penser que	*it's wishful thinking that*
cela met en doute	*that calls into question*
le phénomène paraît difficilement explicable	*it seems hard to explain the phenomenon*
dépasser la compétence de	*to exceed the capabilities of*
ce n'est que la partie visible de l'iceberg	*this is just the tip of the iceberg*

9 Whatever your views, the opposite side of the argument needs to be given an airing:

regardons de plus près le revers de la médaille	*let's look closely at the other side of the coin*
il faut bien reconnaître que	*it must be recognised that*

la contrepartie de	*the opposing view of*
l'un n'exclut pas l'autre	*the one does not exclude the other*
tomber dans l'excès inverse	*to go to the opposite extreme*
il en est de même pour	*the same thing applies to*
venons-en maintenant à	*let us now turn to*
selon les antagonistes de ce point de vue	*according to opponents of this point of view*
d'autres faits qui méritent d'être mentionnés sont	
	other facts which deserve a mention are
un autre argument frappant souvent avancé	*another striking argument often put forward*

10 And you need to sum up and reach a reasoned conclusion of some sort:

quelles conclusions tirer de... ?	*what conclusions can be reached from ... ?*
tout semble indiquer que	*everything would seem to point to the fact that*
tout pousse à croire que	*everything leads us to believe that*
à en juger par	*to judge by*
on ne peut pas se contenter de	*we cannot be satisfied with/we cannot just*
il faut garder un sens des perspectives	*we must keep things in perspective*
être# à même de	*to be in a position to*
être# en bonne voie de	*to be well on the way to*
il est évident, d'après ce qui précède, que	*it is clear from all of the above, that*
c'est un phénomène de mode	*it's a passing phase*
il s'ensuit que	*it follows from this that*
on est tenté de conclure que	*it is tempting to conclude that*
on pourrait bien se demander si	*one might well wonder whether*
en fin de compte	*when all's said and done*
toutes choses considérées	*all things considered*
en définitive	*when all the arguments have been heard*

MOTS ET PHRASES DE LIAISON

à jamais	*for ever*
à tel point que	*to such an extent that*
absolument	*absolutely*
actuellement	*now*
apparemment	*apparently*
approximativement	*approximately*
au contraire	*on the contrary*
au fond	*basically*
autrefois	*in the past*
autrement	*otherwise*
bien entendu	*naturally*
bref	*in short*
cependant	*however*
certainement	*certainly*
complètement	*completely*
considérablement	*considerably*
d'ailleurs	*moreover*
dans un sens	*in one sense*
davantage	*more*
de plus	*furthermore*
de toute façon	*in any case*
désormais	*from now on*
du moins	*at least*
effectivement	*in fact*
en aucun cas	*on no account*
en fait	*actually*
en moyenne	*on average*

en outre	*besides*
en principe	*in theory*
en revanche	*in vain*
évidemment	*obviously*
généralement	*generally*
heureusement	*luckily*
là-dessus	*thereupon*
naguère	*in the past (recently)*
naturellement	*understandably*
néanmoins	*nevertheless*
notamment	*in particular*
or	*now then*
par conséquent	*as a result*
par la suite	*subsequently*
parfois	*sometimes*
pourtant	*however*
principalement	*mainly*
probablement	*probably*
quant à	*as for*
quelquefois	*sometimes*
sinon	*if not*
soi-disant	*so-called*
surtout	*especially*
tandis que	*whereas*
théoriquement	*theoretically*
totalement	*totally*
tout à fait	*quite, totally*
vice versa	*vice versa*
vraiment	*really*
vraisemblablement	*probably*

LES VERBES SUIVIS D'UN INFINITIF

All the following verbs take an infinitive (e.g. elle s'arrête de manger, il préfère attendre, je commence par écrire, etc.)

accepter de	to agree to
s'acharner à	to be bent on
achever# de	to finish
s'adonner à	to devote oneself to
adorer	to love
aider à	to help to
s'amuser à	to enjoy
s'appliquer à	to apply oneself to
apprendre# à	to learn to
s'apprêter à	to get ready to
s'arrêter de	to stop
arriver à	to manage to
s'attendre à	to expect to
avoir# du mal à	to have difficulty in
avoir# envie de	to want to
avoir# l'intention de	to intend to
avoir# le droit de	to have the right to
avoir# raison de	to be right to
avoir# tendance à	to tend to
avoir# tort de	to be wrong to
brûler de	to long to
cesser de	to stop
chercher à	to attempt to
choisir de	to choose to
commencer# à	to start to
commencer# par	to start by
compter	to plan to
consentir# à	to consent to
consister à	to consist in

se contenter de	to content oneself with
continuer à	to continue to
contribuer à	to contribute to
décider de	to decide to
se décider à	to make up one's mind to
se dépêcher de	to hurry to
désirer	to wish to
détester	to hate to
devoir#	to have to
empêcher de	to prevent from
s'empresser de	to be anxious to, to hasten to
encourager# à	to encourage to
s'engager# à	to undertake to
espérer#	to hope to
essayer# de	to try to
éviter de	to avoid
être# en train de	to be in the process of
être# sur le point de	to be about to
exceller à	to excel in
finir de	to finish
finir par	to end up by, to finally ...
forcer# à	to force to
s'habituer à	to get used to
hésiter à	to hesitate to
s'impatienter de	to long to
inciter à	to urge to
s'intéresser à	to be interested in
inviter à	to invite to
se lasser de	to be tired of
menacer# de	to threaten to
mériter de	to deserve to
mettre# (une heure) à	to take (one hour) to
se mettre# à	to start to
négliger# de	to neglect to

111

nier	*to deny*
obliger# à	*to compel to*
s'occuper de	*to deal with*
offrir# de	*to offer to*
omettre# de	*to omit to*
s'opposer à	*to oppose*
oser	*to dare to*
oublier de	*to forget to*
parler de	*to talk about*
parvenir# à	*to manage to*
penser	*to intend*
perdre# du temps à	*to waste time*
persister à	*to persist in*
se plaire# à	*to delight in*
préférer#	*to prefer to*
prévoir# de	*to plan on*
prier de	*to beg to*
promettre# de	*to promise to*
proposer de	*to suggest*
refuser de	*to refuse to*

regretter de	*to regret*
renoncer# à	*to give up*
se résigner à	*to be resigned to*
se résoudre# à	*to make up one's mind to*
réussir à	*to succeed in*
rêver de	*to dream of*
risquer de	*to risk*
savoir#	*to know how to*
sembler	*to seem to*
servir à	*to be used as/for*
songer# à	*to consider*
souhaiter	*to wish to*
tâcher de	*to try to*
tarder à	*to be slow to*
tenir# à	*to be keen to*
tenter de	*to try to*
trembler de	*to be afraid to*
venir# de	*to have just*
viser à	*to aim/intend to*